MUSINGS OF A
BUDO BUM

by Peter Boylan

Copyright © 2017 by Peter W. Boylan

Cover art by M. Richard Frye. Interior photographs by M. Richard Frye and Grigoris Miliaresis.

All rights reserved under International and Pan-American Copyright Conventions. Published in the United States of America

First Edition: February 2017

Print ISBN: 978-1-48359-868-0

eBook ISBN: 978-1-48359-869-7

CONTENTS

THANKS

I want to thanks to all the people who contributed to help make this book a reality. Without the support of many backers, this book would have remained a dream. In particular:

Padraic Hallinan

Eric Tilles

Nick Lowry

David Allgeier

Zdenek Dvorak

Bob Mooney

Markus Hansen

Jun Akiyama

Bram Intix

I must give special thanks to Deborah Klens-Bigman for all of her help editing essays and asking excellent questions about my ideas that drove me to deeper understanding that I would not have achieved without her critiques and questions. I also want to thank Rick Frye for his superb photography and artistic skill in putting together the cover. Many of my students have helped through asking questions and allowing me to experiment ideas with them, including Charles Ham, Rolf Granlund, Patricia Anderson, Scott Watson. Over the years, many friends have argued with me, hit me in the head with sticks, proven to me I was completely wrong, and otherwise helped me explore budo ideas. Thank you Chuck Gordon, Emily Gordon, Wendy Gunther, Jim Baker, Janet Rosen, Adam Grandt, Martin Kelley, Neil Simon, Shaunton Davis, and Al Panackia. I am surely forgetting to mention someone, and if it was you, I'm very sorry.

INTRODUCTION

I've been practicing *budo*—Japanese martial arts—for thirty years. When I started, well before the advent of the Internet, I had little idea of what I was getting into. I'd seen kung fu on TV and I'd read some magazine articles, but looking back, I really had no idea what I was getting into. I walked into the college judo *dojo* in 1986. Since then, I have been blessed with many gifted and talented teachers in Kodokan Judo and the other arts I have stumbled upon in my journey.

At the time, Earl Bland and Bob Noble were teaching the classes and leading the judo club at Western Michigan University. They gave me my first taste of what budo could be. I had some ideas about what it meant for something to be "do", a Way, 道, but that was from having read *The Tao Of Pooh* and a couple of mediocre translations of the *Tao Te Ching*. I had a lot to learn about the difference between what I imagined a Way was, and what practicing one really means. Earl and Bob started me on the path and gave me my initial lessons about how to fall down and how to get up again.

Eventually, I graduated from college and found a job teaching English in Japan. In Shiga, I was welcomed into a wonderful *dojo* in Omihachiman lead by Yoshikawa Toshimi and Hikoso Kunio. These gentlemen took in a very rude, unmannerly young stranger and accepted him into the *dojo* for training. I must have been a challenge to have around. My Japanese was minimal when I first walked in, and I thought I knew a lot more than I really did. I will always appreciate their patience in not throwing me out for being too much trouble. They put up with me and slowly taught me some manners while broadening my understanding of what a Way is.

While working in Japan, I stumbled upon a swordsmith while riding my bike home from getting a haircut. Nakagawa Taizoh welcomed my curiosity and invited me in for a cup of tea. This was the beginning of one of the great friendships of my life. He introduced me to the beauty and majesty of Japanese swords. Through him, I was able to handle blades of incredible beauty and age. We would sit up late having discussions about everything imaginable, and when the topic was Japanese arts and history, he would happily cut my misconceptions to shreds while the cats wandered across the room and over the sword blades he was working on. He lit in me a desire to really understand Japanese swords and pushed me to explore the culture of budo to a depth I hadn't realized was possible.

Toward the end of my first stay in Japan, I somehow stumbled across an iaido (iai) *dojo*. I went to a festival celebrating an old castle. Even in Japan, a group of people swinging swords in *hakama* and *uwagi* is an unusual sight. For me it was amazing. After their demonstration, I managed to get myself introduced to the leader, Takada Shigeo. He was a tall, gray-haired gentleman with powerful shoulders and a warm, welcoming manner. He invited me to come to his *dojo* and learn iai. This was the answer to the dream I'd had since getting to know Nakagawa *Sensei*. To fully appreciate a Japanese sword, I felt that I needed to understand how to use one. Contrary to the myths about the classical arts that I had absorbed, Takada *Sensei* was happy to take me in as a new student. He introduced me to the world of *koryu* (classical, pre-1868) budo, the old schools of budo founded before the end of the Tokugawa Shogunate in 1868.

Takada *Sensei* introduced me to his *kohai*, Kiyama Hiroshi, a man with such a powerful demeanor that it was only after I had known him for a long time that I realized that he's only about 5 ft (152 cm) tall. When Takada *Sensei* passed away, Kiyama *Sensei* kindly took me into his *dojo* and continued teaching me Muso Jikiden Eishin Ryu. It was quite a *dojo*, with three different lines of Eishin Ryu being practiced and shared, as well as kendo and other fun stuff. Kiyama *Sensei* also taught me Shinto Hatakage Ryu Iai Heiho, an art form on the brink of extinction, with only two practitioners before I began studying it.

During a break at iai practice one day, I noticed one of the teachers, Kohashi Michiko, doing some work with a stick in the corner. I was seized by the thought that I had to learn it. She introduced me to her jodo teacher, Hashimoto Tatsushi. Hashimoto *Sensei* started teaching me and introduced me to his teacher, Matsuda Shigeharu. Matsuda *Sensei* started teaching me the *koryu bugei* Shinto Muso Ryu. Through him, I met other legendary Shinto Muso Ryu teachers such as the late Kaminoda Tsunemori.

Each of these teachers has given of themselves to help me understand and progress along the way, and this book is dedicated to each of them.

GETTING STARTED

We all have to start somewhere. Most of us start with a collection of impressions and myths we've picked up from movies and television, and maybe some magazine articles or books. That's where I started. Since then, I've had a lot of myths and misconceptions. Living far from the home of budo in Japan, as most of us do, getting accurate information has always been a challenge. I hope that these essays will start to replace some of the myths with clear information. There are essays about where you can get good training, the role of etiquette in the *dojo*, how to use all those titles you see properly, and what those ranks mean.

Figure 1Naginatajutsu at Kashima Shrine. Photo copyright Grigoris Miliaresis, 2014

DO YOU HAVE TO STUDY IN JAPAN TO UNDERSTAND BUDO?

I have written this essay in an attempt to give a reasonably complete answer to a question that comes up with fair frequency. I would say that it is possible to truly understand budo without training in Japan but that this is in truth very difficult. There are a few teachers out there who might be able to impart the whole contents, but not many. In the USA, I'm thinking of people like Phil Relnick, Ellis Amdur, Wayne Muramoto, and Meik Skoss that might have a shot at doing it, but it's tough. Budo is not the technique. It's everything else. The techniques are really a vessel for carrying all the things that are budo: the values; the customs; the expectations and behaviors; the honor, duty, and loyalty; the way of thinking about things; and the way of interacting with the world as you move through it. These all make up what budo is; to think that by learning techniques and *kata* you are learning budo is a great mistake. Budo is vastly more.

So what is budo if it's not the techniques? The word is made up of two characters, *bu*, 武, and *do*, 道. Often it is a wild goose chase to try and figure out the intention of Japanese words by taking apart the kanji characters they are written with. Many words are of ancient vintage, and their actual usage has changed so much that relying on the kanji to give you the key to understanding is a mistake. The important thing is how the word is used in the language today and not how it was used hundreds of years ago when the word was first written.

In a way, this is true of budo as well. It is often used to simply mean "martial arts" in everyday usage in Japan. For example, if you check the Kenkyusha Online Dictionary, it gives the following definition:

ぶどう¹【武道】(budo) martial arts; military science;

By this definition, boxing is budo, fencing, Thai kickboxing, sambo, and many other martial arts. I will admit that it is a definition I have heard used in popular conversation and media in Japan. Anything that trains one in some sort of combat is budo. If this is what you are interested in, then you've probably read enough and can skip the rest of this essay. On the other hand, in conversation within the budo community in Japan, the usage is different, much more complex, and nuanced. This is the meaning that I'm concerned with.

This more complex meaning is one that includes budo with a number of other cultural practices in Japan. Practices like *sado* (茶道) *kado* (花道), *shodo* (書道), and *kodo* (香道) are known in English as tea ceremony, flower arranging, calligraphy, and incense smelling, respectively. Yet, like budo, they all contain that "do," 道. What we have is an entire class of activities that are "do," but what is "do"?

"Do," 道, is a character meaning "road, path, or way," and it goes back to the ancient Chinese concept known as Tao or Dao. There are two primary sets of writings that provide the foundations for what has become known as Taoism in English. The first is a small collection of eighty-one brief poems that can be read in less than an hour. Best known as the *Tao Te Ching*, there is a decent translation at http://academic.brooklyn.cuny.edu/core9/phalsall/texts/taote-v3.html. These are the foundation writings on the Tao. The other set of writings are by Chuang Tzu. There are several translations on the Web and many published translations as well.

The Tao is a good place to start. The first chapter of the *Tao Te Ching*, the oldest writings about it, says (Footnote 1):

> *The tao that can be told*
> *is not the eternal Tao.*
> *The name that can be named*
> *is not the eternal Name.*

> *The unnameable is the eternally real.*
> *Naming is the origin*
> *of all particular things.*

> *Free from desire, you realize the mystery.*
> *Caught in desire, you see only the manifestations.*

> *Yet mystery and manifestations*
> *arise from the same source.*
> *This source is called darkness.*

> *Darkness within darkness.*
> *The gateway to all understanding.*

If "the tao that can be told is not the eternal Tao," then explaining the Tao is going to be tough. Merriam-Webster's *Collegiate*

Dictionary gives us, "the unconditional and unknowable source and guiding principle of all reality as conceived by Taoists," which is actually a good start. Tao becomes the source and origin of everything. So if we can bring ourselves into moving and acting in one with the Tao, we will be in harmony with the universe and our actions will be correct.

In the story of Cook Ting from the writings of Chuang Tzu (the second great set of writings on Tao), it is shown that any activity can be practiced as a means of achieving an understanding of the Tao. Ting is a cook in the kitchen of Lord Wen-Hui. When asked about his marvelous skill, he replies, "All I care about is the Way. If I find it in my craft, that's all." Cook Ting uses his craft as a vehicle for finding and deepening his understanding of the Tao. This is not necessarily an intellectual understanding, for he says, "now I go at it by spirit and don't look with my eyes. Perception and understanding have come to a stop and spirit moves where it wants. I go along with the natural makeup, strike in the big hollows, guide the knife through the big openings, and following things as they are." (Footnote 2)

This is the simplest base upon which all of the various "do" are built, whether it is sado or shodo or kado or budo. The goal is to use the craft you are practicing to come closer to the Tao and to remove the barriers between ourselves and the Tao. This is what we are trying to do when we practice any "do". We are trying to achieve a closeness and understanding of the Tao, the universe, the origin of all things, through the practice and development of our craft, our art.

If you watch a really good *kendoka* or *judoka*, they don't seem to be fighting an opponent. They seem to just move naturally and without apparent aggression, and their partner's actions are nullified. They move again and their partner is defeated without them having taken any real action. I know I have felt this at the hands of some of my judo teachers. We are moving around the mat and suddenly I'm airborne. My teacher hasn't done anything dramatic. His movement seemed to naturally place him in a position where a technique happened. He didn't throw me. Everything came together so I was thrown more by my own action than anything my teacher was doing. He was just there and I was moving in such a way that I bumped against his hip and went flying.

This is the little goal of budo. You strive to be so in harmony with the essence of your art, with the world, and the Tao that things happen without your doing anything. This is a principle concept of the *Tao Te Ching* known as *wu wei* (無 為). In action, the master *kendoka* or *judoka* doesn't appear to actually do much of anything and yet is victorious. Chapter 38 of the *Tao Te Ching* says:

The Master doesn't try to be powerful;
thus he is truly powerful.
The ordinary man keeps reaching for power;
thus he never has enough.

The Master does nothing,
yet he leaves nothing undone.
The ordinary man is always doing things,
yet many more are left to be done.

The bigger picture is to expand this mastery and understanding of a small, limited field to life and achieve this same understanding and oneness with the Tao in all aspects of life so that everything one does is effortless and perfectly in harmony with the world around them.

The idea of the Way is not limited to Taoism, however. One of the classics of Confucian thought, *The Great Learning*, begins:

大學之道、在明明德、在親民、在止於至善。

The way of great learning consists of manifesting one's bright virtue, loving the people, and stopping only when perfection is achieved.

Tao is a critical element of the Confucian and Neo-Confucian thought that was a major influence on Japanese throughout their history. In Confucian teaching, Tao was more focused on human affairs and making the right decisions naturally such that it happened without thought. Confucius was focused on society and human affairs, so when he writes of Tao, his focus is on its importance at that level. In Neo-Confucian writings, the focus is more on the cosmic significance of Tao. However, in all of them, Tao is a critical and fundamental concept for understanding the world, our place in it, and how we should develop ourselves and live in the world. In addition, when Buddhism arrived in China, the concept of Tao was appropriated to describe many ideas in Buddhist teachings as they were translated into Chinese. As a result, everywhere one looks in classical thought, you find the Tao and its related ideas.

The *Tao Te Ching* and *The Great Learning* are texts that have been the fundamental to the educated in China for thousands of years and in Japan since the writings was introduced from China around the fourth century CE. They are just the first, and shortest, of the many writings that make use of the concept of Tao that were considered an essential study for any educated persons in Japan up to the end of the Edo Period in 1868. These concepts were used to explore and conceive everything from ideal social order and relationships to the cosmos. Budo, and the Ways that preceded it, sado, shodo, and others, were all the province of the educated classes in old Japan.

At one point, someone commented that budo is "nothing special." I agree that budo is nothing special. In Japan, that is. The techniques you are practicing and the craft you are learning are just tools for practicing all the "do," 道, aspects. Much of what the "do" is, is embedded cultural knowledge that Japanese take for granted as shared cultural and historical knowledge and experience. Outside Japan, we don't have that basic cultural and historical knowledge, so what is ordinary and a given in Japan, is exceptional and unknown outside Japan. This is true whether we are talking about budo or any of the other cultural traditions of Japan. The teachers outside Japan must have a thorough understanding of these cultural elements to be able to fully impart their budo. For a foreigner training in Japan, these elements smack you in the face so often that you learn them almost as organically as the Japanese do growing up. When training outside Japan, the teacher has to consciously include them in the instruction. It can be imparted across cultures, but the teacher has to understand what elements beyond the techniques have to be taught as well for a student to fully grasp the "do" portion of budo.

In my experience, very few teachers outside Japan have made the effort to educate themselves about the cultural matrix in which budo is embedded and relies on to give the teachings their full context and relevance. Budo training that includes that understanding is such a rich and deep experience that it makes training without it seem like eating a paper plate at a picnic instead of the food on the plate.

I'm not trying to suggest that budo teachers outside Japan have become experts on Taoist and Confucian philosophy. That is a life's work by itself, and there are precious few Japanese budo teachers who are also masters of philosophy. Most Japanese teachers have a native cultural understanding of the concepts that they have absorbed from living in Japan. For a teacher outside Japan, I think some reading of the classic texts on Taoism and Confucianism along with plenty of quiet thought about how they relate to budo practice is probably enough. Quiet thought fertilized with the ideas of Lao Tzu, Chuang Tzu, and Confucius should bring about some profound realizations on the nature of practice and what the great teachers who created the Ways hope for us, their students, to achieve.

Footnotes

1. All quotes from *Tao Te Ching* are taken from S. Mitchell's translation at http://academic.brooklyn.cuny.edu/core9/phalsall/texts/taote-v3.html on October 14, 2013.

2. Cook Ting quotes from http://www.bopsecrets.org/gateway/passages/chuang-tzu.htm.

ETIQUETTE: FORM AND SINCERITY IN BUDO

For a lot of people outside Japan, Japanese *reishiki*, or etiquette, seems quite heavy, stylized, and empty. There is so much of it in Japanese life that people who live in a low etiquette society such as the USA assume that it must involve just empty motions that don't do much other than to make the people at the top feel good about being at the top. Japanese groups appear to move in scripted scenes that don't leave any room for human feeling and individuality.

This isn't quite true, but it does take a little while to get familiar enough with how things are done to be able to read what is being done and said through the language of etiquette. Traditionally in Japan, and by this I mean during the Tokugawa Period (roughly 1600–1868), much of life was strictly controlled and people worked very hard to make sure they behaved within well-known and carefully ordered norms. Getting your etiquette right was critical. It could quite literally be a matter of life and death.

Lord Asano was being instructed in proper Edo court etiquette when he lost his temper, drew a dagger, and attacked the instructor, Yoshinaka Kira, setting in motion Asano's sentence to commit *seppuku* and his followers on the path of vengeance that led to Yoshinaka's death and their immortalization in the tale of the 47 Ronin. Getting etiquette right was that important. One version of the events holds that it was because Asano felt he was not being properly instructed that he became angry. Whether this is true or not, the fact that it was plausible enough for people to accept it as motivation shows how critical etiquette was.

Thankfully, people in Japan don't place quite as much importance on etiquette as they did in Asano and Yoshinaka's time, but it is still extremely important, and people watch how others practice their etiquette quite carefully. Now it is about expressing respect; giving courtesy; and honoring people, places, and practices.

In the *dojo*, formal etiquette serves several purposes beyond just the social. It provides structure, a clear understanding of proper behavior, a means of expressing respect and appreciation, and a way of maintaining a safe training environment, among others. While there can be quite a bit of variation in etiquette between various martial arts, and even between *dojo* that practice the same art, it's not that difficult to understand the basics. Etiquette is really about expressing respect for people and ideas.

We take off our shoes and bow when we enter the *dojo*. This shows respect for the art that is practiced in the *dojo* and maintains the basic function of keeping the floor clean and minimizing the amount of time required to clean it. The *dojo* is a specially designated space for practicing arts that teach horrific combat skills while also refining students' minds and bodies. The bow shouldn't be tossed off like it's a bothersome requirement. It's a chance to show that you appreciate the art, the person who is teaching it to you, and your fellow travelers on the path who enable your learning by offering themselves as training partners as well as your respect for the seriousness of what you are learning. These are certainly things worth a second or two to express your appreciation for. Watch the people who regularly just toss off a head bob and come barreling in without a thought for what they are doing. Do they treat their partners in the same thoughtless manner?

The bows that open and close *keiko*, the training itself, are similar. They are chances to express your appreciation for the founder of the art you practice and all the teachers down to your own are sharing with you. You're not just going through a moldy old Japanese ceremony. That bow is a chance for you to think briefly about what practicing the art means for you and to express it through your action. If someone is watching, they should be able to tell that you care about what you are doing. You shouldn't look like you are only doing it because you have to do it before you're allowed to train.

The other big piece of etiquette that is common across all Japanese arts is bowing to your teacher and training partners. I'll be honest; it's a lot easier not being Japanese in a *dojo* in Japan, for Japanese bowing can be a carefully calibrated activity. How deeply they bow is dependent upon what their social status is relative to the person they are bowing to. This can get complicated fast, but the basics are that the lower your status compared to the person you are bowing to, the deeper you bow. So you bow relatively deeply for your teacher, more deeply for her teacher, and very deeply for the head of your art. In Japan, people pay close attention to this, and many businesses will give new employees classes to be sure they are doing it right and don't offend any customers. There are some wonderful videos on the Internet of women in kimono demonstrating a variety of different bows to be used when greeting persons of varying social status, and doing so perfectly. They aren't that difficult to find [footnote 1].

Not being Japanese or in Japan, we don't have to worry about getting just the right angle and depth of our bows to express the precise degree of relative social rank. We should still bow with sincerity though. We can take a tenth of a second required to make it more than just a motion we go through and turn the bow into an expression of how much we appreciate what we are learning from our teacher. If we are bowing to a training partner, it's a chance to show our thanks that they will let us train using their body. It is all too common for people to forget that our training partners are making us a gift of their bodies. They are trusting us to train using their bodies and to not damage them while we are learning. That's a huge gift and deserves a sincere expression of respect. Don't make the bow perfunctory.

These are the major points of etiquette in all the budo *dojo* I've trained in. We bow when we enter the *dojo*. We bow at the beginning of practice and again at the end. We bow to each person we practice with. Different arts will have more elaborate customs than this, but I can't imagine any Japanese budo that will have anything less.

Many iaido systems include a bow to the sword at the beginning and end of training. Considering that a genuine *shinken* is an extremely expensive work of art comprising the efforts of several master artisans, and that it will outlast any individual user by a thousand years or more, it seems appropriate to express respect and gratitude to the makers and to the instrument they created that we have the opportunity to train with for a short while. Some aikido *dojo* make a point of bowing to their *bokuto* and *jo* when they take them out and put them away. Many *koryu* systems have special bows for beginning and ending *kata* practice that show respect for the opponent and partner but simultaneously indicate complete focus on them as a threat.

There are lots of variations on the basic theme of expressing respect and courtesy, but the basic format of bowing into the *dojo*, bowing at the beginning and end of practice, and bowing to your training partners never seems to vary. If you do this with the clear and sincere intention of showing respect and honor and if you sincerely strive to be courteous, I have found that people tend to overlook honest mistakes. If you are sincerely trying to be polite and follow the local etiquette, regardless of how new and different it may be, people will appreciate the sincerity and help you get the details right the next time.

It's very easy to see when someone is not sincere about the etiquette, and people will only treat you with the respect that you express in your etiquette. If showing respect in your etiquette is too much of bother for you, and you insist on slouching through it, people will take this as a sign of your lack of respect for them and what they do and will treat you accordingly.

First and always, *dojo* etiquette should be sincere. The formal etiquette serves many purposes beyond providing a way for people to show respect for each other but it is always about showing respect and appreciation. This is true even for those incredible, aggressive bows the *koryu* folks do. If you don't show respect when you bow in with them, they are likely to let you know how they feel about being disrespected, and it won't be a comfortable experience.

I only get to bow to my teacher a few times a year now because I live six thousand miles away from him. When I do get to spend time with him, I want everything I do to express my respect for him as a teacher, my appreciation for what he has taught me, and my love for him as a person. There is no room for stiff, empty form with all that within my heart. Kiyama *Sensei* will be ninety years old this year, and I know that each visit could well be the last chance I will have to express these things to him. With all those feelings driving my etiquette, there is nothing stiff or empty in the etiquette between us. Instead, each bow and interaction is filled with warmth and appreciation. I use all my actions to show my appreciation and respect.

Etiquette, or *reishiki*, isn't about putting teachers on pedestals or for controlling students. It's about showing respect for the people you are learning from, the partners who are helping you to learn, and the art you are learning. There is nothing there that isn't worth showing sincere respect for. If you don't sincerely respect your teacher, the people you are training with, and the art you are practicing, you shouldn't be there. Budo etiquette is about showing everyone how much we respect, appreciate, and honor what we are doing and those we are doing it with.

Note: There is a good video at https://www.youtube.com/watch?v=0p7TrOWgRvo

SENSEI, KYOSHI, HANSHI, AND *SHIHAN*: BUDO TITLES AND HOW (NOT) TO USE THEM

You see and hear a lot of different titles in Japanese martial arts. Unfortunately, a lot of people have little or no idea how these titles and honorifics are actually used. I've seen people addressed as "Smith *Sensei*," "Bob *Sensei*," "*Sensei* Smith," and "*Sensei* Bob." I've also seen people insisting on being addressed as *Hanshi*, *Shihan*, *Soke*, *Shidoshi,* and *Shidoin.* In Japanese budo culture, only one of these is correct.

Being introduced as *sensei* is fine. Introducing *yourself* with a title sounds either ignorant of its Japanese usage or extremely arrogant, as if you are giving yourself an honorific. If you are introducing yourself, it's just "Peter *desu*" or "Lowry *desu*." Anything more is arrogant or foolish. Even the very senior *Shihan* of my acquaintance just introduce themselves with their names. Their business cards will have their ranks and certificates, but that's all; no honorifics. Those are things other people use to talk about you, not something you use for yourself. Certificate titles like *Shihan* or *Shidoin* aren't forms of addressing either.

Sensei isn't a title. It's an honorific like "Sir" or "Lady." In English, it would be a little strange to introduce yourself by saying "I'm Sir Boylan." It's even stranger in Japanese, where the honorific a person uses to address you depends on your age, position relative to the person addressing you, the particular situation, and your relationship with them. I have been addressed as everything from *kun* (a diminutive used to show that I'm a lot lower in status than the speaker), to *san* (the general honorific used for people of relatively equal status), to *sama* (shows great respect and implies high social status).

Sensei is a mild honorific. It means "teacher," and everyone who teaches gets called it, regardless of whether you are teaching biology or swimming or *kenjutsu* or skateboarding. The eighty-year-old, Nobel Prize-winning physics professor and the sixteen-year-old skateboard teacher are both *sensei*. As is, I should add, any doctor and any politician. Do you really think being lumped in the same category as politicians is all that wonderful?

Many people are fond of trying to find deep meaning in the characters used to write Japanese words. I don't get too excited over how words are written in kanji. The writing was decided a thousand years ago or more, and the actual day-to-day usage has shifted since then. Much more important is how the word is actually used in Japan now than how someone decided to write it a millennium or more ago.

If you teach English in Japan "*Eigo no sensei*" isn't too bad a way to describe yourself. It's a job description. However, "*Eigo no kyoshi*" would be more in keeping with standard Japanese usage. *Sensei* is a title used to address people. *Kyoshi* is a title used to describe a position, like "plumber" or "teacher" in English. *Hanshi, Shihan, Shidoshi,* And *Shidoin* are also titles to describe a position or certification. These are not terms ever used to address someone directly. Using them in conversation would be like walking around a university campus and addressing the instructors by their official university titles like "Hello, Professor Smith"; "Good afternoon, Assistant

Professor Nakamura"; or "Good evening, Adjunct Instructor Rosen." It sounds quite strange.

Another point to note is that you don't generally say something like "I am X's *sensei*." You'd say, "X is my student." It's one of those cultural nuances.

I can't think of anyone who puts *Sensei* on their business cards, and without trying to sound pompous, I've got quite a few business cards from eighth *dan* and various *hanshi* and *shihan*. (If you hang out in budo circles in Japan for any length of time, you'll accumulate a few. It's just a normal part of the social interactions. It doesn't suggest that you actually "know" anyone or have any significance yourself.) If you have an organizationally awarded title such as *kyoshi*, *hanshi*, or *shihan*, you would put that title on your business card. It's like putting "Ph.D." on your card. It's a title that an institution has awarded you. You aren't claiming that anyone should use it in addressing you. Usually, it's added along with a listing of *dan* rank, such as *Nanadan, Kyoshi* or *Hachidan, Hanshi*. That sort of thing. I've never seen *sensei* on a card though.

This is how such honorifics and titles are used in conversation. *Sensei* is a title like Mr. or Mrs., but since it's Japanese and we're doing Japanese arts, it has to go *after* the person's name. Please show a little awareness on this and don't tell me, "This is America." I know it's America, but we're practicing Japanese arts, so get the usage right for the art you're practicing. If you're boxing or wrestling, whatever is standard in those activities is appropriate for those activities. If you're fencing or doing savate, you use the forms appropriate for them.

Using honorifics and titles incorrectly is a red flag. If someone is claiming rank or claiming to teach Japanese budo and they aren't getting simple things like proper use of honorifics and titles right;

this is a big warning sign. It doesn't take much to learn how these things should be used. If someone is using them incorrectly, it suggests to me that they really don't have any experience in Japanese budo. So please, show that you know as much about the etiquette of the arts as you do about the techniques, and use the titles and honorific forms of address properly.

DIFFERENT RANKS IN MARTIAL ARTS?

I got involved in another discussion about the real importance and value of rank. This conversation has been around since probably the day after Kano Shihan established the now-popular system using black belts and ten steps of rank (known as *dan* [段]in Japanese). You'd think I'd be over this discussion, but I can't seem to let it go by without taking another whack at it. I'm sure there were huge discussions within the Kodokan, because the rank system there evolved over several decades before it was finally settled in the form we are all familiar with.

The question of what a particular rank means can be an interesting one. People are constantly asking, "What is a black belt?" and "What does rank really mean?" These questions need to be looked at in connection with a couple of other questions. Those are, "What is a *sensei*?" and "What is a student?"

In the world of classical Japanese martial arts, the *koryu bugei*, these questions don't seem to exist. It might be because people are not evaluated in comparison with each other's level of attainment. They only give scrolls that correspond with the portion of the system you have learned and teaching licenses that lay out what you are qualified to teach. This only leaves one question to ask if you are talking to a possible teacher, and one to ask anyone you are training with. The question for possible teachers is, "Are you licensed to teach?" and the question for training partners is, "Can you do this technique or *kata*?"

For me, part of the issue is that I've been in the iaido and *koryu* worlds for a long time. I started in judo, and I still train, but I spend a lot of time in other arts. The Kendo Federation (where I got my iai and jo *dan* ranks) has ranks, but there are no symbols of rank. Everyone in the room dresses alike, from the guy who just started, to the eighth *dan* who's been at it for more than eighty years. The *koryu dojo* I'm in are even less fussy about the ranks and such. Yes, you get some such certificate sometimes, maybe a license, but that's pretty much it. There are even fewer signs of rank there than in the Kendo Federation. The fascination with belt colors is only in the judo and karate systems, and something that is big outside Japan. In Japan, you get a black belt comparatively quickly, and all it tells people is that you are a real member of the club who can take the *ukemi*.

This leads back to the initial questions, "What is a *sensei?*" and "What is a student?" These seem obvious. A *sensei* is someone who teaches, and a student is someone who learns. Those answers work fine in a standard school classroom setting, where most questions have right and wrong answers. The kids sit at the desks and the teacher stands in front of the whiteboard. They don't work so well in *dojo*, where everyone mixes; the teacher might be in her thirties or forties, and the students are anywhere from nine years old to ninety-one, and even the teacher is working to improve her understanding of the art.

The student's role seems straightforward. The student is there to learn the art. To do that, the student is responsible for showing up healthy and ready to learn, with a good attitude. The student is responsible for herself. That was quick and easy to write, but it's not very satisfying. Showing up healthy is pretty simple. Budo is practiced in close contact with other folks, so please take responsibility for yourself and don't expose your training friends to every illness you get. Stay on the sidelines when you're sick. .

So what is a *sensei*, and what is she responsible for? This might not be a complete answer, but what is a *sensei* needs to be considered before we can go any further. I'll start by disappointing everyone who wants to break down the Japanese word 先生 and define it by its parts. We don't understand the modern meanings of English words because their original German, Greek, or Latin roots meant something different a thousand or two thousand years ago. We define them based on how they are used today, and the same goes for Japanese. In Japanese today, *sensei* is used to address a teacher, doctor, lawyer, politician, or any important person. Most commonly, it just means teacher. Nothing more. It has no fancy, special, abstract, or mystical meanings. It just means teacher. The word doesn't help us.

In a budo *dojo* though, the *sensei* doesn't do a lot of classical talk and chalk teaching. *Keiko* in a budo *dojo* is a different situation from teaching an academic subject in a classroom, with different concerns, conditions, and goals. The teacher has responsibilities to the students and to the art she is teaching. I'm partial to the modern version of *koryu* budo instruction rather than the military style instruction that became popular in Japanese and Okinawan arts during the 1930s and 1940s in militarist Japan, which continued and spread worldwide afterward in *gendai* (modern) budo such as karate. *Koryu* is generally done in smaller groups, with more personal instruction and less regimentation. This reflects what a *sensei* is responsible for.

A *sensei* is responsible for students having a safe training environment; that should go without saying, but it doesn't, so I say it often. This is *koryu bugei*, and one significant difference I've found between *koryu bugei* thought and practice and nearly every other teaching situation I've seen is that, in *koryu bugei*, the *sensei* has no responsibility for making sure students learn anything. The *sensei* is responsible for making sure students can learn if they make the effort. If someone doesn't make any effort and doesn't learn anything, that's the student's issue.

In both *koryu bugei* and *gendai bugei*, the *sensei* is not only responsible for teaching the student. The budo *sensei* is responsible for the art as well. They are responsible for passing on the entirety of their art to the next generation. They are not responsible for popularizing the art and teaching it to as many people as possible. In fact, many senior members of *koryu bugei* systems view trying to spread an art as being an abdication of their responsibility to the art. Trying to spread an art quickly risks having poorly or incompletely trained people teaching and not doing a good job of teaching, and worse, corrupting the art because they don't understand it well enough.

The lessons of any good budo system, *koryu* or *gendai*, are far more complex and deeper than just the movements. In addition to the physical movements, there are strategies and tactics for controlling the spacing between you and your opponent. There are techniques and concepts for controlling yourself and your mind. Much of a budo system is beyond physical movements, and constitute the real heart of a system. Without a proper understanding of these aspects, an art cannot truly be taught or learned. The responsibility of the *sensei* to the *ryuha* includes making sure that only students with an adequate understanding of all parts of the system are teaching. It is better to remain small and obscure yet pass on the entire system than to grow into a huge, globe-straddling organization that teaches only a mere shadow of the original art. The teacher's responsibility to the art is greater than to any individual student.

Interestingly, it's strange how quickly most students begin to see and understand this. The art, the system, dates back generations: *koryu bugei ryuha* can be more than 500 years old, and Kodokan judo, the exemplar of *gendai* budo, is over 130 years old. The *ryuha* (system/school/art) has its own priorities, requirements, and benefits. These outweigh the needs of individual students. As students develop an understanding of the deeper nature of the teachings of the *ryuha*, they also understand that the *ryuha* will continue long after them and that their responsibility is to learn the system to the fullest of their ability so that those who train with them and follow them will learn the full system in its entirety and none of it will be lost or corrupted.

Students who begin to understand this also begin to see and take on responsibility for maintaining the system. Mastering the art is no longer just about gaining personal skill. It becomes about being part of a larger structure that stretches back into history and pushes on into the future. As students move from being beginners to experienced students to teachers licensed to teach a portion of the system and occasionally become licensed to teach the entire system, their rank isn't about status. It's about responsibility. The higher your rank, the more responsibility you have to the system. Students who are only interested in learning the system for themselves and who don't take responsibility for the system should be, and usually are, slowly frozen out of the school and sometimes even simply expelled.

This is the way it should be. As I've been reading more about the early days of the Kodokan and the new rank system that Kano Jigoro *Shihan* implemented, and it's evolution, it becomes clear that in the early Kodokan, rank—at least at the early to middle levels—instead of being based on how well they knew the whole of Kodokan Judo, was strictly about how well they could fight. Students were promoted when they defeated four people of the same rank. I suspect that this caused a not-so-subtle twisting of priorities among the growing membership of the Kodokan. We can see the effects today in the way the International Judo Federation values competition above all else and downplays or ignores the other 90 percent of the Kodokan syllabus. What has happened is that, in many modern budo, rank has simply become a symbol of competitive accomplishment and not a reflection of system mastery or responsibility.

This leaves me with the sad reflection that we have two different answers to the question of rank. The first is, "What should rank mean?" It should be a reflection of a student's mastery of the system and their responsibility to it. The second question is, "What does rank actually mean?" In *koryu bugei*, rank is still a reflection of a student's mastery of the system and their responsibility to it. In *gendai* budo, sometimes rank is a reflection of a student's mastery of the system and their responsibility to it, and sometimes it is a recognition of the student's competitive accomplishments. Figuring out which is which usually isn't too difficult.

ZANSHIN

気を付ける、残心、中心する、意識, 無心, *ki wo tsukeru,* *zanshin, chushin suru, ishiki, mushin,* paying attention, staying alert, being focused, and awareness are all terms that everyone has come across in budo training. Some, like *ki wo tsukeru* and *zanshin,* are heard regularly, while others aren't heard as often but are just as important. Budo is all about physical technique though, so why should we spend our time on mental areas like these? Physical technique is great, but it is the mind that is the true weapon, and how we train it is even more important than how we train the body.

Many of the things that change average technique to great technique are not technical. They are mental. Doing things like controlling timing and spacing begin with mental awareness and focus. I don't care how good your technique is; if your timing or spacing are off, the technique is worthless. Understanding timing and spacing is mental. It's about awareness and focus. This is where practice gets interesting. Learning another armbar variation or another way to do *kirioroshi* frankly doesn't teach you very much that can be applied anywhere except in the very closely defined realm in which it is learned.

Learning to let go of all the stuff cluttering up your mind so you can pay attention, stay alert, and be focused and aware of the world is tough stuff. I'm still learning how to do it. One of the peculiar things about budo practice is that correction is usually really fast when you lose focus and let your alertness, your awareness, go. I've gotten hit in the head more than once because I wasn't paying proper attention. The physical practices should lead us into the mental ones.

In budo, we often talk about *zanshin* (残 心) and *mushin* (無 心) You'll notice that the last character is the same in both words. It means heart/mind and represents "the psyche; the mind; the emotions" (definition from the Kenkyusha Online Dictionary). In *zanshin*, the first character is for something that remains, that is left, that stays. The idea is one of staying aware, staying alert, your mind focused on the situation at hand. In *koryu bugei*, as well as in kendo and many other modern budo styles, the idea is that the *kata* doesn't end when the action ends.

You have to stay aware and focused even after the fight is over. Even though you have ostensibly won, you can't just relax and lose your focus. The action might not be over yet. What if your adversary has friends who come along suddenly? Or what if the adversary isn't quite finished? If you just relax, drop your guard, and start thinking about how glad you are that the fight is over, you won't be surprised prepared for what comes next. The Muso Jikiden Eishin Ryu *kata* called Yaegaki a great example. The *kata* assumes an adversary directly in front of you. Once she has been overpowered, you start to sheath your sword. When it's almost all the way back in the *saya*, the adversary rallies to take a swing at your leg. If you have relaxed, you won't be able to respond in time to save your leg. If you are still aware, if you are practicing *zanshin*, you can.

All *koryu bugei kata* that I am aware of requires that the student practice maintaining awareness, *zanshin*, even when the action is over.

Really though, the training is to be aware well before the action starts. In kneeling *kata* like Yaegaki or the much less complicated

Mae, the *kata* doesn't begin when the action starts. It begins the moment you start to kneel. In paired *kata*, such as in *kenjutsu*, the *kata* starts as soon as you bow to your partner, and it doesn't end until you've moved apart and bowed to signal the end. I have memories nearly as vivid as the bruise I got one day when my attention wandered after the action of a *kata* was finished and my partner, the instructor, recognized this and caught me in the solar plexus. I had dropped my attention because we were "done." Except that we weren't. We were still close enough together to be immediate threats, and I should have been maintaining *zanshin*. I wasn't, it was clear to my partner, and he gave me a gentle reminder.

Zanshin is focused awareness, but it's not so narrowly focused that you forget about the rest of the world. You have to be aware of what is around you at the same time that your attention is focused on your adversary. This is the mental extension of the <u>metsuke</u> that I wrote about previously. With *metsuke*, you want to keep yourself focused on your adversary, but you can't lose your peripheral vision and awareness of your opponent. If you only look at his weapon, you miss what he's doing with his body. If you only look at his face, you don't know what he's doing with his weapon. The saying in budo is *enzan no metsuke* (遠山の目付), or roughly, "looking at a far-off mountain." The idea is that your gaze is focused on one point, but your peripheral vision is still active and taking in the whole of the scene. In budo, the point is that you are focused on your partner but you can still see his entire body and weaponry in your peripheral vision.

This focused awareness, in my experience, is something like this. Your attention is fully focused on your partner, but you are still aware of your surroundings as well. In the *dojo*, you don't want to move into the way of another group who are also training, you don't want to run into a wall, and you don't want to hit anyone you aren't training with at that moment. I first experienced this type of awareness at judo practice. During *randori* (open grappling practice, in this case), the mat would be filled with grappling pairs, most standing, and a few on the ground. I had to be completely focused on what my partner was doing while at the same time being aware of the people around me on the crowded mat.

At first, I had trouble just keeping my attention on my partner. I would drift back into my own mind thinking about what to do and immediately get thrown. I didn't have enough awareness to encompass my partner and the rest of the people on the mat. Fortunately, my partners generally did. Gradually, my ability to focused improved, and then my awareness started to expand. I learned to be aware of the world around me without taking my attention off of my partner

This is a part of *zanshin*. You have to maintain your focus on your partner without losing your awareness of the rest of the world. In solo iai practice, the reasons for this can be made explicit; the adversary may not be finished, or there may be other adversaries still around. It's more difficult to model this in paired *kata*, but the aikido training technique of multiple attacker *randori* can do a good job of this. You have to remain aware. *Zanshin* 残心.

This whole line of thought was kicked off by a piece I read in which the author talked about trying to make a list of things to do while she dusted the *dojo*. As dusting didn't require her focus or real awareness, she tried to do other things like make to-do lists with her awareness. One of the long, slow lessons I have taken from studying budo is to do only whatever I am currently doing. I don't have enough awareness to spread it out to multiple activities and do any of them well. The more I practice just doing one thing at a time and being aware of what I am doing, the better I get at it.

This is a lesson that is not only unique to budo but is also fundamental to any of the Ways. In fact, it's one that is probably better taught in other Way traditions such as shodo and sado than in budo. In calligraphy and tea ceremonies, the practice of focusing on what you are doing and only on what you are doing is right up front. In budo, it's awfully easy to get tied up in the cool techniques and dealing with an opponent and forget to be focused and aware of what we are doing.

Zanshin is helpful in just about anything we do, even simple, mundane tasks such as dusting. I find that the simple tasks get done faster and better when I am mindful of what I am doing. If I let my mind go flitting wherever it pleases, I miss details of what I'm doing and end up doing a poor job. But the other benefit of doing simple tasks mindfully is that I am practicing being mindful and aware of what I am doing. The more I practice this with simple tasks, the easier it becomes with more difficult, complex tasks (like trying to catch the *tsuka* of the sword while the swordsman is trying to hit me with the sword). And the better I get at mindful awareness in the *dojo*, the better I am at applying it throughout the rest of my life.

That's the thing about training in a Way, whether it is budo or sado or shodo or kado or any of the others. The training is not just about the particular isolated skill of fighting or making tea or writing pretty characters or arranging beautiful flowers. It's training for all of life. In this case, it is training our mind how to approach and deal with any task, to be focused and aware of what we are doing, but not so absorbed that we forget the whole world. We have to remain aware.

BUDO

Budo is a journey, not a destination, but what kind of journey is it? This section is about the nature of budo. Budo covers a lot of territory. From *kata* training to the responsibility that comes from being proficient at violence, this section looks at what it means to train in budo. What happens in the *dojo* and how do you relate to the people you train with? How does training reshape your relationship with the world?

Figure 2: Chigirikijutsu demonstration at Kashima Shrine.
Photo copyright Girgoris Miliaresis, 2014

DO VERSUS *JUTSU* (道 対 術)

The whole Do versus Jutsu discussion only gets played outside Japan. It's something that Donn Draeger came up with and presented to the world. It was an interesting idea, but frankly, he was wrong. There is no opposition between the two concepts. To have a Way ("Do" [道]) you must have skill (*Jutsu* [術]) to build it from. In order for skills to be coherent, they must be organized in a Way. Do is founded on Jutsu, and Do also makes sense of Jutsu.

It is not "either–or." It is "both–and." Either–or is something Westerners insist on. It used to make my teachers in Japan smile at my ignorance when I pressed this conversation on them. Both together. One without the other just doesn't make sense.

When we start, we tend to focus on the skills, because we need them as a foundation to understanding what the Way is. Beginners can talk about the big picture and the fundamental principles, but these have to be explored and experienced through the practice of discrete skills and techniques. These provide the map to understanding the Way and the principles of the Way.

The *do* idea is a really old one in Japan. Sado (茶 道) or tea ceremony has been called sado since at least the time of Sen No Rikyu (the sixteenth century), and there are martial arts being called *do* that I have seen going back to at least the seventeenth century. Even the founder of Kodokan Judo, Kano Jigoro Shihan, recognized that the term *judo* had been used by some groups long before he started using it.

Historically, most arts were known simply by their name (Hayashizaki Ryu, Kashima Shinryu, Shinto Muso Ryu) without adding an adjective such as *jutsu* or *do* prior to and during the Tokugawa Era. Names and descriptions changed often, but the organizing principles did not. Separating a technique from the principles that make it work is, to my mind, impossible. Having a principle without any applications or techniques that express the principle is difficult to imagine.

Ideally, the principles give rise to the techniques, and the techniques point the Way to the principles. Some great masters had deep insight into the principles of their art and developed techniques that express this principle. The circle begins with the master having an insight into the principles and developing techniques based on those principles, that Way (道). Students then study the techniques as way of learning to understand the principle behind them. The techniques serve as road markers along the path to the principles, the Way that underlies the art. The students master the techniques and come to embody the principles and express them spontaneously. They then begin teaching these techniques to a new generation of students. The circle thus continues.

In Japanese, there are a lot of terms that express the concept of the Way: *michi* 道、*houhou* 方法、*kata* 方 (different from the *kata* meaning from 型、形). The goal of any art, whether it is described as *jutsu* or *do*, skill or way, 術 or 道 , is that the practitioner can express the principles of the art/school/style/system spontaneously in accordance with the situation. If you only learn a collection of techniques, but don't understand the principles that underlie the techniques, you will only be able to use them in the exact situations in which you learned them. If you use the techniques as tools for learning the underlying principles, the Way, then once you begin to understand the principles, you will be able to apply them to all sorts of situations, not just the specific one covered in the technique you learned.

In a fully developed martial art/martial science, the principles and the techniques cannot be separated from each other. The techniques work because of the underlying principles, and the principles are expressed through the techniques.

WHAT *KATA* ISN'T

Let's get this straight. Classical martial arts *kata* are not practice fighting. They are not what fighting is or was. Martial arts *kata* do not simulate combat conditions. They do not recreate actual combat scenarios. If *kata* aren't any of these things, then what are they, and why bother with them?

Kata are pre-arranged training sequences. *Kata* are training scenarios for learning about essential elements of conflict. I train in both classical and modern Japanese martial arts, and both use a lot of *kata*. Classical arts tend to focus almost entirely on *kata* training. *Gendai* arts like judo use a combination of formal *kata* training, *randori*/sparring, and informal *kata* that are usually called something else.

Kata are not for mimicking combat . *Kata* are for getting better at conflict. They are a training tool for learning the skills necessary for dealing with combat. They are an exceptional tool that has survived hundreds of years of testing and application. As a training tool, they provide a framework for practicing various aspects of combat, not just repeating techniques or practicing in a sparring situation where much of what is effective is not acceptable because of the risk of injury.

Kata is not sparring, and with good reason. All sparring assumes a dueling scenario: two people faced off and fighting. Any equipment is equal. There are no surprises, no unexpected changes. There is an assumption of fairness. *Kata* is not handicapped by any of these of these assumptions. *Kata* allows a much broader investigation of conflict conditions.

Classical martial arts *kata* generally start out simple, but they rarely assume anything is fair or equal. Araki Ryu Kogusoku is famous for one of the first *kata* taught to its students. It assumes asymmetrical armament (the *tori* has a tray, and the *uke*, a tanto) and applies the element of surprise to defeat the better-armed opponent [Footnote 1]. There is nothing fair about this situation. It is unfair and tricky and applies deception. Just like a lot of conflict in real life. Sparring is worthless for learning these lessons.

The *kata* of Kodokan Judo, unlike the games of Olympic Judo, rarely assume anything is fair or balanced. The *Kime No Kata* is a great example [Footnote 2]. It is a set of *kata* of encounters between two people. One person, always unarmed, is attacked in sequence in a variety of scenarios. First the two are kneeling facing each other, as if talking, and one, *uke*, attacks the other in a variety of unprovoked and basically surprise attacks. The *uke* attacks from the rear. After, that a succession of attacks with a knife from the front and side. Then they stand up and there are unarmed attacks from the front, side, and rear, followed by attacks with knife, stick, and sword.

Sparring is extremely limited in so many ways that *kata* is not. In all of these jujutsu *kata*, the only thing the person being attacked, *nage*, in judo terminology, knows is what attack is coming. They don't know when, or how fast, or from what range, or how strong the attacks will be. *Uke* has complete control over these.

One complaint sparring enthusiasts often make about *kata* is that you always know what attacks are being made, so it's never a surprise. The same is true in sparring as well. In sparring, a very small set of techniques are allowed, and the vast majority of possible attacks are excluded under the rules. Moreover, in sparring, the attacks are always coming from the front, eliminating 75 percent of the directions the attacks come from. With it representing such a tiny fraction of possible encounters, sparring seems quite overrated as a training method for anything except sports encounters.

Another thing *kata* isn't is completely prearranged. *Kata* leave a lot of room for changes in range, timing, and rhythm. In *koryu bugei* systems, the *uke* is always supposed to be the senior, more experienced person. It's the job of the *uke* to control the speed of the *kata* so their partner is always learning and being pushed into new territory. In addition, just because the *nage* knows exactly which attack is coming doesn't mean handling the attack is easy. No one tells the *uke* when he has to attack. Uke gets to decide the exact moment of the attack, its speed, and intensity. I have had *uke* drive me completely helpless just by drawing out the attack a little bit and then drawing me into responding at a different rhythm and speed than they attack with. This left me wide open with a big stick incoming at speed and I was unable to do anything about it.

Kata isn't locked into one interpretation. The job of the *uke* is to adapt the *kata* speed, intensity, and range to the student's level so they learn as much as possible from the training. *Kata* also isn't locked into just one *uke*. If you train with many different *uke*, each will bring different things to the training, things that make each practice of the *kata* unique. Different sizes, heights, strengths, speeds, and levels of experience in each *uke* all combine to change the *kata* every time you do it.

Kata isn't some dead, fossilized thing that you trot out to see how things were done at some time in the past. *Kata* are vital and alive and being changed and adapted all the time. No one says you and your partner can't decide to try the *kata* differently and see what an appropriate response would be if you change one element. For advanced students, that's a great thing to try. The creation of *kata* isn't over either. People are creating new *kata* all the time. Most new *kata* don't end up being preserved and passed on, but sometimes the *kata* have enough value that they are added to their system. The histories of styles like Eishin Ryu and Shinto Muso Ryu show how things were added to these systems through the centuries. *Gendai* budo do the same. Kodokan Judo didn't create the Kodokan Goshin Jutsu until the 1950s. Over time, *kata* get tested, and the worthwhile ones are kept and passed on, while the others are dropped and forgotten.

Kata are a teaching method for practicing the most fundamental and important aspects of conflict. They are part of a time-tested method that allows you to practice all sorts of dangerous attacks and defenses in a controlled manner. *Kata* allow attacks from every angle at all sorts of speeds and force levels, and they allow that practice in all sorts of asymmetrical matchups. *Kata* give practitioners the opportunity to practice these matchups at a variety of speeds, strengths and intensities, so they can grow, and their skills progress.

Note 1. The Araki Ryu *Kata* mentioned can be seen at https://www.youtube.com/watch?v=n2_Z-whRDRk

Note 2. The Kime No *Kata* can be seen at https://www.youtube.com/watch?v=BZz2ERlRKIY

TRUST IN THE *DOJO*

Trust is a wonderful thing. Real trust is something that is earned over time. In budo practice, trust is absolutely essential. What we do in the *dojo* can't happen without it. We are practicing dangerous, potentially crippling, or even fatal techniques. We have to practice them on our partners, and we have to turn our body over to them so they can practice. We have to expose ourselves to incredible physical vulnerability so our partners can practice. In a very real sense, we are loaning them our bodies so they can learn. In turn, they do the same for us. Without fuss, without complaint, seemingly without concern, they turn their body over to us to practice throws, strikes, joint locks, weapons attacks, and all sorts of things which are simply dangerous and could get them seriously injured. When we're in the *dojo*, it seems perfectly natural.

When I think about the amount of trust I give to my partners, and how little I even think about it at this point in my training, it's really amazing. I don't think twice about letting someone throw me, twist my wrists so the bones in my forearm cross, turn my arm so my elbow is taken in an unnatural direction, or assault me with large sticks. It's what I do now. I can't believe I trusted training partners so much or so easily back when I started out on this path.

Trust, real trust, the deep down kind, the "here's my body; go ahead and throw it around a room" kind, the "hit me with that stick" kind, isn't something you give naturally. I have to remember back a long way to when I started Kodokan Judo and began letting people throw me and armbar me and choke me. I was stiff for a while.

Absolute trust in my partners did not come right away. I had to work at it with them. The first people I trusted were my teachers. They could pick me up and put me down and it felt even safer than diving into my own bed.

Trusting my peers, especially my fellow beginners, was different and took a lot longer. We had to work hard together, and go through more than a few bumps and bangs as we learned to throw and to be thrown. It's scary when someone who knows as much as you do, which is nothing at all, picks you up and then hurls you at the ground. No wonder beginners are stiff. They are trusting some stranger to not break them horribly. Over time, students learn to trust their partners not to hurt them, and they learn to trust their own skills to receive the techniques safely.

I know that I trust the people I train with regularly a lot. A lot more than I trust people that I spend significantly more time with. Based on the amount of time we spend together, and that fact that we do what we do as much for the enjoyment it gives us as for anything else, it's surprising how much I trust these people. I freely hand them my body to do with it pretty much as they please, without any worry at all. In many ways, I trust them vastly more than I trust most of the people in my life.

This level of trust has been earned. I train with these people often, and the training environment is one where people's fundamental nature becomes remarkably clear remarkably quickly. As I train with people, the vast majority of them are fundamentally good. You quickly realize who is a little careless or a bit thoughtless when they are training, because these people hurt their partners more often and don't realize that they are doing it. There are all sorts of personality quirks that show up quickly when you're handling people and doing dangerous things with them. The ones who are careless or thoughtless get extra instruction about that in the *dojo*, and they are genuinely upset and apologetic when they do something wrong.

There are some real diamonds in the *dojo* too, people who go out of their way to be helpful and willingly absorb extra pain while you work on a technique that is giving you problems. They are also the folks who are quick to work with beginners who have no control, which makes beginners dangerous regardless of how wonderful a person they are. They are also wonderful to let work on you because of their care and the honesty of their technique. They aren't hiding anything; there is no hidden agenda and no secret desires.

The folks who aren't nice but usually cover themselves with at least a civilized veneer in conversation and outside the *dojo* don't seem to be able to hide anything in the *dojo*. The guys who get a kick out of hurting people or who like to prove how powerful they are show their true colors when training and they get a reputation pretty quickly. There are the guys who always crank an armbar harder than it needs to be, and they always seem to hold the technique for a while even after their partner has tapped to signify that the technique is effective. Nobody likes these people, and nobody trusts them. They show who they are very quickly. They muscle their techniques and they throw extra hard so their partners hurt when they get up.

This is why I trust the people I train with so much. We are operating at such a raw level that people's true natures are nearly impossible to hide. We give our training partners immense power over ourselves. We routinely give them the power to hurt and injure us. We know who will be petty and mean enough to hurt us more than absolutely necessary, who might be basically good but a little careless, and who is a truly wonderful human being. In the *dojo*, we play with raw power to harm people, and the ones who enjoy hurting others can't hide this from us. Then they lose the trust that everyone else in the *dojo* has for each other.

I've seen a few of these guys over the years, and they happily trade the trust and community of the *dojo* for the feeling of power they get when they abuse a partner or when people are afraid to work with them. They seem to think this makes them strong and powerful. They are always on the outside of the *dojo* community because no one really trusts them, regardless of how good their technique becomes.

I trust the people I train with so much because it is so easy to spot the rotten apples and avoid them. Better yet, the best *dojos* I've been in simply don't tolerate their behavior. They either shape up and play nice, or they are encouraged to leave. I just don't tolerate them in my *dojo*. I love the people I train with because time and time again they have proven that I can give them my body to do with as they please and they will give it back to me whole and healthy. In fact, I often have to tell them to be a little bit stronger, to hit me a little bit harder, because they really don't want to hurt anyone and they perform the technique less than completely because they don't want to cause me the little bit of pain that goes with it. We trust each other because we know each other at the fundamental level where we have the power to harm and we know what the others heart looks like there.

It's amazing how true this is even when you visit a new *dojo*. After working with a person for just a few minutes, you will know more about their personality than you would in days of working with them outside the *dojo*. There are so many opportunities for someone of ill will to take advantage during budo training that in under fifteen minutes I can tell if someone should be avoided.

What is wonderful about going to a new *dojo* to visit is that the vast majority of people are very good, and they show it clearly when we train. After an evening of training with a group of people at a new *dojo*, I have a new group of trusted friends, because we have shared ourselves with each other, and shown that we care about each other's wellbeing. Training means operating at a fundamental level where we offer ourselves to our partners and they show who they really are by how they treat us while they train. It's hard to find an activity outside the *dojo* where you do something with such a powerful exchange on a regular basis.

The trust that this builds is a wonderful thing.

TRAINING

Budo is training. We train to instill the principles of our art in our bodies and minds. How we train is important. Good training moves us forward, poor training can be more like being stuck on a hamster wheel; we work really hard but don't get anywhere. Bad training can be dangerous, leading to injuries that set back our progress and even make training impossible. This section is about how we can train more effectively, and some mistakes I've made along the way that I hope you can learn from without having to repeat them.

Figure 3: Naginatajutsu at Kashima Shrine. Photo copyright Grigoris Miliaresis 2014

TRAINING, MOTIVATION, AND COUNTING TRAINING TIME IN DECADES INSTEAD OF YEARS

Budo, like any Way, is certainly a lifetime activity. There are quite a few teachers in Japan with seventy or eighty years of training under whatever is left of their belts after all those years. In comparison, I'm still just a beginner, with something over twenty-five years of budo training. I'm still excited to go to the *dojo* every practice though. What is even more surprising is how excited I am about training again when practice is over. I bounce with excitement and enthusiasm. (No, really. I'm known as Tigger in some circles.)

Practice is clean. Whatever I did the last time I was in the *dojo* doesn't matter. The only thing that counts is what I'm doing right now. That alone is a great feeling. Each practice is an opportunity to create something new out of myself. I go in and don't have to worry about the baggage of work or finances or other commitments. In the *dojo*, the only commitment is to my training and my training partners.

We should all be there for similar things. We want to train hard and correctly. We want to maximize the effectiveness of our technique through optimal body mechanics as well as mastery of timing and spacing. We want to learn effective technique. We want to polish both our physical and our mental skills.

There are days when I really want to train hard and push myself physically and other days where I'm completely wrapped up in the mental aspects and may not even break a sweat. Training offers a variety of aspects of myself that I can work on. There always seems to be something worth working on that brings me into the *dojo*, and the longer I train, the more things there seem to be for me to work on. With all the different facets of budo that need work, I can always find at least one that I want to polish any given day.

I started budo in a college judo class in 1986. I wanted to learn about Chinese philosophy in action, and that was the closest thing I could find. I had some vague ideas from having read the Tao Te Ching but I really didn't know what I was getting into. Though I smile at some of naive ideas I had back then, I really could have done a whole lot worse.

That class introduced me to budo. Everything was exciting and fascinating and really, really difficult. I had to repeatedly learn how to walk, move, and fall down. I mean really, who needs to learn how to fall down, right? But that was the very first lesson, and it's one I'm still working on. Oddly enough, it's still the one practical lesson I've used more than nearly any other. I'm clumsy, so I still fall down a lot, but I will admit, I use the walking lessons slightly more than the falling lessons.

Any good budo has so much more depth than just learning some effective fighting techniques (but if the base isn't effective combat techniques for the situations being studied, then it can't be budo). Effective combat techniques are the first step, but all the really fascinating stuff happens after that first step. Being effective is just the beginning. That's why really masterful *budoka* seem to have magic powers. They didn't stop studying at just effective. They kept polishing and learning, making their effectiveness more and more efficient, until it looked like magic.

For me, the wonderful thing is that everything is still exciting and really, really difficult to do right. As I progress in the arts I practice, there is no level that is "good enough" because getting "good" isn't the point. The point is continuous improvement. I have had teachers in their nineties who still practiced regularly and were working on improving right up until their bodies gave out.

My teachers were, and are, still learning, still making progress, and still improving. That's a great challenge. It's also a wonderful realization. It means I'm never finished growing. While I live, there will never be a point when I am finished, a point when I am done. That fact, that knowledge, that I am not complete, and that I can always get better is a fabulous motivator. I can't ever say "That's just what I am." Because I know it's not. It's only what I am now. It's not what I'll be tomorrow.

It's a wonderful feeling to know I always have capacity for growth. That's my real motivation. Yes, I'm working on cleaning up my *kirioroshi* these days, and yeah, I noticed that my foot is flaring out on some techniques so I'm working on correcting that. Little puzzles are there all the time. Every once in a while, I manage to tie a bunch of them together and make a large leap all at once. Those are great feelings, but I don't really pursue them. I just appreciate them when they happen. What keeps me coming back are the little steps forward, the small epiphanies, the knowledge that, to quote a good friend, I can suck at a higher level tomorrow.

Budo is gratifying that way, and it doesn't matter how much time I have to give it. There have been times when I was able to train five or six days a week. There have been times when I have had to fight to get one practice a week in. These days, I'm usually getting two or three practices a week in, plus some weight and cardio training to keep the old body in good operating condition.

There is one other thing about budo that I love. That's the fact that it's not really about martial arts. The martial arts are just the container. Budo is really about developing and improving and mastering the self as a human being. That's what being a Way, a 道, is about. If you just want to learn to fight, there are faster, simpler, more stripped down ways to it, not necessarily more effective for fighting, but certainly more efficient for learning.

I'm motivated to get up and go to the *dojo* because it helps me be better at being me. As I said, I know that what I am today is not what I am. It's only what I am now. Practicing budo teaches me about how to refine my physical and mental budo technique. These are lessons I apply directly to the rest of my life. I know that if I can learn to not let *uke* play mind games with me in *kenjutsu* or jodo, that if I can learn to not let my opponent get under my skin and cause me to lose control during judo *randori*, I can learn to do those things outside the *dojo*.

Budo is the container for the lessons, but the lessons are universal. This is true of any *do*'s, 道, but I find it to be particularly true of budo. In budo, we deal with conflict at its most basic level. Whether it is unarmed or with a sword or a staff or *kusarigama* or a spear or some other exotic weapon, we're dealing with conflict. The techniques for dealing with conflict in a particular system of budo seem to be specific to the particular situations that are practiced. In the case of many *koryu* budo where the training is with archaic weapons, the lessons might not seem to be relevant to anything anymore. The principles for dealing with conflict haven't changed though. They can be applied to any sort of conflict, whether it is has devolved to physical conflict or not.

Even if budo didn't go any higher than teaching principles for conflict, it would be fascinating. You've got the physical practice which challenges me every day, and which I expect to continue being challenged by for another forty or fifty years. Then you've got the mental level of learning to work on with partners and opponents. Above that are the fundamental principles of conflict that you can learn and discover ever more subtle depths to. This might well be enough to keep me motivated and occupied for the rest of my life. That's just the "bu," 武, portion though.

Beyond "bu," there is the "do," 道. That's a big motivator for me. The lesson that gets drilled home every time I practice is that I don't have to be satisfied with myself. I don't have to settle for being no more, no better, than I am today. The lessons of budo give me a path, a way, for becoming better so that I will suck at a higher level tomorrow. With budo, I get to do this with some great people in lessons that challenge me on every level: physical, mental, and spiritual.

Those people are another motivator for me to drag myself into the *dojo* even when I'm not feeling up to it as much as I can. They help me and push and pull and sometimes drag me forward. There is tremendous camaraderie in the *dojo* that is refreshing and simple. I like these people and I like being around them. I trust them and they trust me. In the *dojo*, we have a wonderful time together practicing something that can be deadly serious. Having wonderful people to train with really does help pull me back even when I think I'm too tired.

I'm not sure these are the same things my teachers are getting out of budo now. I know that my reasons for training shifted subtly over the years. At first it was Chinese philosophy, and then I really liked learning the techniques and skills of fighting. For quite a few years now I've been focused on refining my budo and myself. Looking out at the next few decades of training, I wonder what other things might motivate me in the future.

THE MOST EFFECTIVE MARTIAL ART

I think this needs to be said, and said often: The effectiveness of a martial art should be judged not by what the most gifted practitioner of the art can do with it but by what the least gifted practitioner can do with it.

When people talk about how great a martial art is, the reference point used is almost always what the very greatest of practitioners of the art can do. These are inevitably fabulous and gifted martial artists. In general, they can do incredible things I will never be able to dream of doing. I've felt this level of skill first hand. Judo is one of the arts I study, and because it is an Olympic sport, who is the very best of the best among the competitors is not open to argument. I've had the good fortune to train with Olympians and world champions. I know what their skills and arts feel like. (They are almost undetectable. They are generally so subtle you only realize you've been thrown when your back hits the floor.)

The vast majority of us don't have their gifts of speed, dexterity, and sensitivity. I've seen that the very finest of martial artists, whether the art in question has a competitive sport or not, exhibit these same gifts of speed, dexterity, and sensitivity, whether the art is unarmed or armed. What this gets to is, that if we compare martial arts by comparing what the most gifted practitioners can do, we may well only be comparing who is the most gifted, and not which art has the most to give.

A lot of people talk about which martial art can beat another in a head-to-head matchup. To me, that's rather pointless because such head-to-head matchups never happen. What I want to know, what really interests and excites me, is what can a martial art do for an average to below-average practitioner. You know, someone like me. This is where things get interesting because now the foe isn't some other highly trained martial artists; it's our own clumsiness.

What will studying the martial art do for me? I already know it won't make me an unbeatable fighter. No amount of training is going to do that for me. I don't have the gifts. But training will do other things for me. Will it increase my sensitivity? Will it improve my timing? Will I gain a mastery at spacing? Am I likely to collect a lot of injuries while training in this particular art? Will I enjoy the time I spend training and feel like it is benefiting me, not just on a physical level but also on a mental level? Will I learn coherent principles that can be applied across a spectrum of encounters and not just a bunch of discrete techniques that can only be used in situations very similar to the ones they are taught in?

Considering these questions one at a time, here is what I get. "Will it improve my timing?" This is a good one that people don't give enough consideration to, in my opinion. "Timing is everything," goes the old line, and that is certainly true in the martial arts. I've seen over the years that the most accomplished, most effective artists—whether in a sportive art such as kendo or judo or in *kata* art such as *kenjutsu* or *jojutsu*—are the ones with the best timing. They attack when the conditions are optimum. They don't waste energy; when the opening occurs, they are there. They move with their opponents and hit their targets with timing rather than speed. I've seen octogenarians completely dominate people in their teens and twenties because they understand timing. They matched their movements with their partner's movements and timed them so they slipped naturally into place.

This brings up the next question. "Will it improve my sensitivity?" Sensitivity includes awareness of a broad range of things. From the closest, feeling and understanding your partner through their touch where they are holding you or your clothes, to your awareness of the world around you and the people in it. At the closest level, I teach students to be aware of their partners even when their eyes are closed, so they can reach out and affect their partner without looking at them or the point they are targeting. From there, sensitivity stretches out to being aware of how someone is going to move and what they are going to do based on understanding the clues in their posture and movement. This requires a visual sensitivity first focused on your partner, and later, as you improve, extending to everything in your awareness. If all you learn to focus on is how to strike or how to see one opponent after they are declared, you aren't learning very much. If you are becoming sensitive to the world around you, you are really learning something worthwhile.

"Will I gain mastery at spacing?" This is a great one because if you can control the spacing between you and a partner, you control the entire encounter. By controlling the spacing, you can limit a partner's options and even choose what options to give them. It's tough to learn about controlling spacing at a range of distances from just one art though. Most arts are very strong at one or two distances. I study Kodokan Judo, which is great at the most intimate distances, the range where you can reach out and hold someone. If you practice some of the *kata*, you can learn about slightly longer distances, the range of hand strikes. It's starts to fall down at kicking ranges and is really bad at weapons ranges. Shinto Muso Ryu Jo is great at a variety of armed ranges, but it has little to offer at the range of touch. You can't learn everything at once, and I wouldn't expect one art to teach you everything. But whatever you are studying, it should spend a lot of time in partner practice so you can learn about spacing. I'm not talking just about sparring, but also partner practice, which includes a lot of slow, careful, thoughtful practice so you can internalize lessons about spacing without developing bad habits.

"Am I likely to collect a lot of injuries while training in this particular art?" This should be a no-brainer, but we forget about it quite often. Is the training atmosphere a safe one? Are these people that I want to be around. Every physical activity has risks (know any basketball players who've had knee surgery?) but the risks should not be excessive. I have friends who have left *dojo* because the way training was run. Usually the problem is not with the art but with the way training is done. Be aware of this. The people you train with have a huge impact on the value you will get from your training and how much you learn. If they don't respect you physically, you could end up badly damaged with injuries that cause lifelong problems. If people don't respect you as a person, you have to deal with not just physical risks, but also with the emotional wear and tear of being treated badly as an individual. Not all injuries are physical. Make sure the particular art in the particular place you are training is safe for you and those around you.

"Will I enjoy the time I spend training and feel like it is benefiting me, not just on the physical level but also on a mental level?" Training takes effort and motivation. If you don't feel like you are benefiting, you're not going to want to do it. Good training should leave you tired, and honestly, exhilarated. The effects should enrich your body through the exercise, your skills through the technical training, and your mind through the broader application of what you are learning. If you aren't getting all three, you might want to rethink what you are doing. I know that when I leave a good training session, I may be so exhausted I can hardly walk, but mentally I am much more alive and aware, and emotionally I am, exhilarated. The training stretches my physical skills and mental awareness so that everything functions at a higher level. This extends to my emotions as well. This is one of the big reasons I love training. It just feels so good at every level.

This is the difference between a coherent art and just a random collection of stuff. "Will I learn coherent principles that can be applied across the spectrum of encounters and not just a bunch of discrete techniques that can only be used in situations very similar to the ones they are taught in?" A lot of people argue over whether something is a Jutsu, 術, or a Do, 道. That's not really a useful question, but I've already written about it elsewhere. The question to ask should be, "Is this based on coherent principles that can be applied beyond the discrete techniques being taught, or is it just a collection of techniques?" The best arts and teachers use techniques as pointers toward principles rather than as an end in themselves. If you are studying throws, do you learn how off-balancing and over-extending contributes to instability in a partner and how this makes powerful throws effortless and effective? If you are studying striking, do you learn how to move your hips and lower body to develop power that can be applied to not only strikes but other movements as well? If you are studying joint locks, are you learning the principles behind locking the joints to prevent movement, or are you just learning to twist the wrist "this way" so it hurts? The art should teach principles that cross all of these areas and that can be applied strategically and tactically as well. Lessons from throwing will apply to striking, while striking lessons apply to joint locks, and lessons about locking the body apply to throwing. The system should be coherent and the principles effective across the range of activity.

All of these things are essential to making a worthwhile art in my eyes. If what you are training in isn't giving you all of these, you aren't getting the most possible out of your art, and the art doesn't do very much for the people studying it. Which art is most effective is the one that does the best job of teaching you the above. Not every art is ideally suited for every person. We each bring our own strengths and weaknesses to our training. The best art will reinforce your strengths and help you overcome weaknesses. It will develop your sensitivity, timing, and mastery of spacing. Your body will be strengthened and energized by your training, and your mind will be polished. You will feel better physically, mentally, and emotionally after training. You will gain skills and understanding that apply far beyond mere physical confrontations.

If you're not getting all of these from your training, you're not studying the best martial art.

THE *DOJO* AS THE WORLD: LEARNING TO DEAL WITH VIOLENCE AND POWER

Budo, like many things, can be seen as a microcosm of life. The *dojo* is a lot like the world. It's a part of the world, so this shouldn't surprise us. What is often surprising is how intense experiences in the *dojo* can be. Activities in the *dojo* are a lot like any other place where people gather to participate in a shared interest. In the *dojo* though, everything seems more focused and intense.

Why should budo training in the *dojo* seem so much more intense than other activities? Maybe it's because, in the *dojo*, we are dealing with essential issues that we sweep under the rug and that polite society tries to avoid or hide rather than face head on. In the *dojo*, we deal with violence and power and force. None of these things are even discussed much in polite society, yet we deal with them all the time. It is considered unseemly to suggest that violence and force are applied in life or that people use power in ways that are bad for those around them.

I've written about trust in the *dojo* before: that trust is built precisely because we are working with these raw building blocks of violence and power and force. Society works to suppress physical violence and expressions of force and naked power. This isn't necessarily a bad thing. I'm pretty sure I don't want to live in a place where these are frequently in play. I like living in a place where violence and physical encounters are rare. That doesn't mean we shouldn't understand them and be able to deal with them.

We train and practice the purposeful application of force in the *dojo*. These things translate into real, physical power and violence. Regardless of the ways in which society suppresses the use of violence, force, and power, they exist in society and are used in a myriad of subtle and not so subtle ways. People use the implication of physical power, or the threat of the use of other power, whether economic or social, to get what they want.

In the *dojo*, violence, force, and power are all out in the open, and we have to learn not only the mechanics of how to use violence and apply power, but how we feel about these things. Some people come in very timid and unsure of themselves and afraid to use whatever power they do possess. Others enter the *dojo* brimming with apparent self-confidence and believing their strength will make them powerful fighters right away. There are people who have had bad experiences being subjected to violence, and sometimes there are people who have been bullies who are looking to enhance their reputation for power. There are all sorts of other folks strung out along the spectrum, each with their own agenda and expectations.

In the *dojo*, we deal with violence, force, and power at their most basic level. If I'm teaching sword or staff work, one of the first things that happens is I tell my student to hit me, and she doesn't. She pulls the cut or strike. So I tell her to hit me again. And again she doesn't hit me. Consistently, new students will pull cuts because they don't want to hurt anyone. This is the most common reaction the first time I ask a student to hit me. Most students have an admirable hesitation to do things that will hurt another person. One part of training is learning to trust their partner, and one part is learning to trust themselves.

Which is harder to do depends on the student. Some of them have learned to be afraid of their own power, so we have to work together until they can commit to trying to hit me without the fear that I will be angry or upset when they do. Mostly there is no problem here. As the teacher in a *koryu* tradition, I'm used to being the beating dummy for new students. They need someone to attack that can safely handle what they are doing. They have to invest the time to develop control and precision. The time this takes varies a lot.

It's wonderful watching students develop. Those who are afraid of their power gradually learn that it's OK to use it in the *dojo*. The *dojo* is a safe place to learn about power. Students take time developing a new relationship with power and violence. One goal is for students who are afraid of their power and any sort of violence to establish a relationship with power and violence that contains neither fear nor domination. Power is a tool, and I want my students to be comfortable with it, but not enthralled with using it.

I do get a few on the other end of the spectrum though, who try wholeheartedly to put me in the hospital with a concussion. Some of them are already brimming with confidence. Some assume that if I'm dumb enough to tell them to hit me, I deserve whatever I get. Some are bringing their own issues to the *dojo* and are just thrilled to have someone to hit. Strangely enough, one of the goals for these students is the same as for the students who are afraid of their power: to establish a relationship with power and violence that contains neither fear nor domination nor an excessive reliance on it.

The *dojo* is a microcosm of life, and it is populated by all the same characters the rest of life is filled with. What is unique is how raw the interactions in the *dojo* are. *Dojo* etiquette can feel unbelievably stiff and strict, but that's because it has to mediate the raw power and violence that is the life of a *dojo*. We see how people handle the etiquette, and we see how they relate to power and violence. We see how they treat their partners, and we learn how they respect others.

This is life in a jar. We get to practice all those encounters we have every day outside the *dojo*, where the power and violence are only implied and suggested, in a place and manner where the power and violence is overt and literally in your face.

That jerk who insists on intimidating people by standing way too close and leaning into people's faces? He's in the *dojo* and he's still trying to push too close and intimidate you. Don't worry about it. Here it's not only acceptable to push him back, it's entirely appropriate, and if you combine it with a gentle whack upside the head to remind him to keep safe *ma'ai*, all the better. The quiet one in the corner cubicle who is always worried about not upsetting anyone and keeps her head ducked down so you can't see her eyes? She's there, and give her all the respect she deserves. Just coming in the door is one of the toughest things she's ever done. That mouthy, arrogant guy who knows he's better than everyone? He's there too, and hide your smile. Yes, he's going to get slapped down repeatedly by the seniors until he learns that he's not better than everyone, but it's rude to show how much you enjoy seeing it happen. The guy who seems to like causing pain and problems purely for the pleasure of being able to cause them? Yes, he's here too, and the seniors will undoubtedly let him know that unnecessary pain and violence won't be tolerated here. They'll probably let him know this and start ratcheting up the amount of pain and violence he receives until he gets the message. All the types of people that you meet in the world come walking through the *dojo* door, bow at the side of the training space, enter, and take part.

So is there anything different from the *dojo* that makes putting up with all of these characters worth the bother? Really, they are bad enough at work or in the gym where they aren't allowed to act out their issues physically, so why would anyone want to put up with them in the *dojo* where they can act upon all the implied violence of polite society? Perhaps because all of us in the *dojo* are working on the same things, whether we know it or not. We are learning to handle our own ability for violence as well as the extent and precision of our own power. Whatever issues we have outside the *dojo* will be clear to everyone in the *dojo*. It doesn't matter what issues we bring with us though; in the *dojo*, we all learn to generate and apply power with precision, whether the application is overt or subtle. Some have trouble using power and violence, while others are completely comfortable with it. The ones who have issues using power and violence gradually become adept at it. Eventually, I don't have to tell them to hit me. They know they can do it, that it's expected, and that it's okay. They become comfortable with their ability to apply power and not hurt me because they choose not to. They get comfortable with being pressured and attacked. The ones who had learned to pressure and attack people outside the *dojo* discover that always pressuring and attacking people may not be the best route. Everyone develops a new relationship with violence and power and force.

Out there in the world, we have to make do applying the lessons we've learned. In the *dojo*, despite having all the same people and issues staring back at us, or perhaps because they are there with us, we are actively working to learn new lessons about violence, power, and force. Both the overly aggressive and the overly timid can learn the same lessons about being discriminating as to when and how much force to apply. We learn to discriminate between when someone is an actual threat and when they are trying to be threatening from what is in truth a weak position. The timid learn that they have power and how to use it. The aggressive learn that being overly aggressive is not a successful strategy. Both are learning when and how to apply force and when not to. They learn how use the power they possess and not place themselves in weak positions.

The *dojo* is the world in microcosm. All the same people and problems are gathered there. The interactions in the *dojo* are intensified because all the issues with power and violence are out in the open and being actively worked with. The wonderful thing is that, in the *dojo*, we are all learning to better understand and appreciate the use of power, force, and violence. We learn when to use it and when not to, what can be successful and what will be ruinous, and when to push back and when to just get out of the way. It's the world in microcosm, but better, because we are learning what to do in the world instead of just stumbling along with whatever lessons life happened to teach us before.

BUDO AND RESPONSIBILITY

Budo is about a lot of things, but one of the least discussed of those is responsibility. The longer we practice, the more important it is that we consider this. At a very fundamental level, in its rawest form, budo is about power. We who have that power are necessarily required to use it wisely. As Stan Lee said so very eloquently through the lips of Peter Parker, "With great power comes great responsibility."

This isn't just about superheroes. As we practice budo, we really do become more powerful. Under normal circumstances, very few people would consider a 5'6" (168 cm), 135-lb (61-kg) woman a significant physical power. Ronda Rousey has been practicing budo for fifteen years though and is an amazingly powerful individual. Her skills give her power. It's a very simple equation. Although many of our social rules and customs exist to keep individual power in check and prevent its abuse, there are plenty of people out there who abuse physical, social, and economic power. There is the office manager who uses his position to bully and take advantage of those under him. There is the rich business owner who uses the power of her wealth to bully people who do business with her. And we all know the physically strong guys who use their power to physically intimidate and hurt people around them.

One of the great things about the power of martial arts skills is how equaling and equal opportunity they are. Martial arts skills make the difference in power between a 135-lb woman and 235-lb man disappear very quickly. I have many vivid memories of small women reducing large guys to lumps on the floor of the judo *dojo* where I practiced in college. Quite often, I was one of the lumps, and whether it was from a powerful throw, a choke, or an armbar, those women impressed their power upon me.

Skill doesn't belong to those who are born faster or stronger or more talented. Skill belongs to anyone who puts forth the dedicated effort necessary to develop it. Once you make that effort though, you get not just that power, but responsibility as well. At the most basic level, once you have power, you have to decide what to do with it. I've seen people become skilled and then become bullies in the *dojo*. I've seen them subtly bully people outside the *dojo* as well. They learned only that they have power. They haven't learned anything about using it responsibly. One difference between just learning a skill, and studying a Way, a *michi*, a *do*, 道, is learning the proper, responsible use and application of that power.

This may be the biggest lesson of budo, larger than all the lessons about technique and *ma'ai* and timing together. Sadly, it's also the most commonly missed lesson. How do we use the power we have? As martial artists, we can easily intimidate and hurt others. After all, inflicting pain and damage is what we are practicing on each other in the *dojo*.

In the *dojo*, we spend a lot of time learning when it is appropriate to use and practice what we know and when it isn't. Japanese martial arts are loaded with rituals that regulate practice so you know when it is OK to try to toss your friend across the room or for her to work on choking you unconscious or for the new kid to try the cool armbar she saw Ronda Rousey do in one of her fights. All that meaningless etiquette and ritual turns out to have some very practical reasons for being there. During practice, there are times when it is OK to work on a technique and times when it's not. There are times when it's dangerous to step on the mat and others when it is safe. There are also considerations of how we treat each other when we are practicing. We learn to treat each other with respect and honor and dignity regardless of how skilled someone is. We are all on the same path, so there is no reason to look down upon someone because they haven't taken as many steps along the path as we have. As we gain skill, our power to hurt and damage increases. That means we are more responsible for not abusing that power by abusing others.

There are other kinds of responsibility in the *dojo* as well. I am not one of those who believe that everyone who advances in rank has a responsibility to teach. There is plenty to do around a *dojo* besides teaching. Everyone can look at their personal capabilities, their powers, and figure out what they should be responsible for.

Responsibility changes as we grow. Once we have the violent power that martial arts training bestows and we recognize the responsibility to act wisely and responsibly, we become responsible for mastering something else. We are responsible for learning the real consequences of using our skills, and not just the myths and irresponsible nonsense like, "It's better to be judged by twelve than carried by six." That's just a flashy cover for the fact that someone doesn't know the real legal consequences of their actions and choices. Knowing those is our responsibility.

This is one of those lessons that stretches out of the *dojo* and into every area of our lives. What are our responsibilities? There are plenty of things that we can do that it would be best not to do. Even though it would be entirely gratifying to apply a joint lock and tie that obnoxious jerk in the next cubicle into a pretzel or choke that other self-righteous jerk into silence, and though it would be a simple and easy application of what we do at practice, we know we shouldn't, and we don't. There are lots of places in life where we have power and we should consider if and how to use it.

We have many different kinds of power beyond the physical power that budo practice endows: economic, social influence, parental, <u>business</u>, and others. We don't often spend time thinking about the responsibility to use the power we have wisely, yet how we wield social and economic and parental power might be more important than how we wield the physical violence of the martial arts. With the power that martial arts gives us, the responsibility not to abuse it is very clear; with other, more subtle forms of power, matters are not always so clear. Sometimes, it's too easy to use power to shoo our kids away when they need some attention but we're a bit tired. It's all too easy on the job to use power to dump work on people or to get out of doing things we should be doing.

This is power too though, and it should be used with consideration and a sense of responsibility as well. If we're really serious about budo, we have to recognize that the lessons extend beyond the door of the *dojo* and impact every aspect of life. Budo is about physical power in its rawest and most basic form, but the lessons about considering when and how it is appropriate to use that power can inform everything we do. Budo teaches many lessons, but how we handle the responsibility of power is one of the biggest.

INVESTING IN FAILURE

Up until last February, I had what I found to be a fairly strong Hiki Otoshi Uchi strike in Shinto Muso Ryu. Then I had the chance to train with one of the senior teachers in our group. I was lucky enough to watch him correct a junior and demonstrate his technique over and over for my fellow student. What a fantastic opportunity for me! As I watched, I could see small differences between how he was swinging the *jo* and meeting the sword and the way I was performing the technique.

Now I'm investing in failure. I could keep doing Hiki Otoshi Uchi the way I have been, which works pretty well. Instead, I've abandoned my old technique as I work to develop the one this teacher uses. The downside of this is that, for now, my technique is lousy. In order to improve my technique and try to reach the teacher's level of smooth, effective control, I have to give up the technique I've developed and start working on something new. For a while, until I begin to grasp the mechanics of this new version of the technique, there are a lot of juniors whose technique will be a lot stronger than mine. I will have to put up with personal frustration as I flub things with the new version I'm working on, things that I could have nailed with my old technique. It's worth the frustration and the flubs and the failures though to develop an even more subtle, effective, and powerful level of skill.

If I can't set aside what I think I know and all the ego and effort that has gone into it, I won't progress beyond this point. I'll be stuck here, unable to advance. On the other hand, if I set aside what I have already learned, take myself back to the practice yard, and treat what I have done in the past as the groundwork that enabled me to see and understand what this teacher is doing, I can make a leap forward. First though, I have to be willing to do what seems like backsliding. At this point, progressing doesn't just mean refining my existing technique. It also means tearing my technique apart and rebuilding it.

To tear a fundamental technique like Kiki Otoshi Uchi apart and rebuild it is not easy, particularly for the ego. For a while, I know my technique is going to be weaker than my students. I am going to be blowing the technique and messing up *kata* practice with horrible and embarrassing frequency. All of the habits developed and laid down so solidly in my neuromuscular system are at war with what I am trying to do now. My old technique was like a good friend. I'd been doing it one way for so long that I didn't need to give it any thought. It just happened. Now if I don't pay particular attention to what I'm doing, it still just happens. I don't want to do it that way though, so I have to pay extra attention to every movement I'm making with my head, shoulders, hands, and hips, all at the same time. Currently I can usually get two or three out of the four to do what I want. The other one or two go back to the way I did it in my old technique, creating interesting hybrid techniques.

The one thing that is consistent about all of these new/old hybrid techniques is that they don't work. Trying to blend them just makes the whole thing fall apart. It will be a few months before I can integrate the new technique into my body and do it consistently. Until I do that, I'm going to be really bad. I expect my students to look at me and wonder if I have lost it. I will feel foolish. A part of me will desperately want to go back to the old way. It's simple. My old technique worked. My new technique doesn't. Yet. For now, I am investing in failure. Instead of doing what worked well enough, I'm going back to being incompetent. I'm wiping the old technique from my system and starting back at the beginning, at the slow, careful, clumsy beginning. This is the only way for me to move forward. I can't build a new, more subtle and effective technique on top of the powerful one I had. I have to let go of what I've achieved so far and become as unskilled as a beginner. Beginners fail a lot. That's why they are beginners. It's also why beginners make such rapid progress compared to those of us who've been around a few years. They haven't accumulated a lot of technique that works well enough that they've become attached to them. They don't have ego invested in being the powerful senior student. They aren't worried about looking like a real teacher. They are beginners and beginners are allowed, even expected, to fail.

For me to make real progress, I have to go back to being a beginner and allow myself to do a lot of failing. It's a check on my progress. If I'm never failing, never making mistakes, I'm not learning anything. Learning is done out there on the edge of our knowledge and understanding, out where we aren't sure of anything except that we don't know. It's not a comfortable place to be. We can't look cool or strong or masterly out there. We can only look like what we really are: students exploring something new that we're not good at. If we have problems with looking like a student, like someone who is learning and figuring out how to do things, we're not going to want to go out and explore new areas of knowledge and understanding. If I'm not failing though, I'm not advancing. It's a little ironic that the best thing to do to improve is to make mistakes. It's only by making mistakes that I can figure out what works better and start on that next step.

So invest in failure. It pays high dividends.

THE SPIRIT OF LEARNING

We study martial arts. That should mean we're here to learn. How we approach learning, the attitude we carry with us in the *dojo*, is critical to what we learn. Sadly, all too often when we get advice, the thought barging through our heads is not, "Thank you. I will work on that." Instead, we're thinking, "I know that. Don't bother me with stuff I already know."

It's easy for me to write that we should always receive advice with gratitude, but what does that really mean? It seems pretty obvious we should appreciate and be grateful whenever someone helps us. That's a lot harder to do than it is to write. So often, people, especially peers—or people who think they are our peers—will give us advice that seems pretty worthless. Advice and instruction can be broken down into three categories. The first and best kind, of course, comes from our teachers. They are giving us advice from their deep experience and knowledge. This is usually easy to receive with gratitude and an open mind. After all, we go to our teachers for instruction on how to perform the techniques right, so whenever they share their knowledge and experience, we are happy to receive it. Except sometimes.

Sometimes teachers are telling us something we already know. Do we really know this stuff though? If we really knew it, would our teachers feel the need to tell us again? For me, the most common direction I get is to relax. After nearly thirty years in the *dojo*, you might think I know I should be relaxed and that my shoulders shouldn't be pulled up tight next to my ears. In one, limited, sense

I do know this, and it's the correction I most often make with my own students. In a deeper sense though, I don't know it. If and when I truly know how to maintain a relaxed state, it will manifest itself in my movement all the time. Kiyama *Sensei* won't feel the need to remind me because I won't be tensing my shoulders and tugging them toward my ears.

Another direction I get frequently from *Sensei* is to use my hips better. Well, what he actually says is "*Koshi ha yowai.*" "Your hips are weak." *Sensei* has been telling me this for years. I'm working on it. I have made major improvements. I can see it in videos of me training in years past compared with now. *Sensei* still pushes this. It's something I know quite well. *Sensei* reminds me often though. Should I feel annoyed with him for always harping on this one thing? Should I be frustrated and resentful that he never lets me forget this?

Annoyance and frustration aren't a part of this. Koshi (腰　), really the whole region of the lower back and hips, are fundamental to everything we do in budo. They are what ties together the foundation provided by our feet and legs with the floating mass of our upper body and head. If this connection isn't solid, my balance will be weak and I won't be able to transfer the power of my legs to my upper body. It's absolutely critical. I've made a huge amount of progress in this area, so why does *Sensei* keep coming back to it? I'm working on it after all. Then I see someone who really gets it, and I wonder why *Sensei* doesn't spend more time pushing on this point.

I approach anything *Sensei* has to say with gratitude and a desire to figure out how to apply what he is telling me. Sometimes, this is pretty tough. I don't always make the connections immediately, so I spend a lot of time wandering around trying to figure out what I'm missing. I learn a lot this way. It makes me think about things from different perspectives trying to understand what *Sensei* is getting at and why it's important at that moment.

It's tougher to take the same advice from someone of equal or lesser skill. Having one of my training buddies tell me to relax or to use my *koshi* could really annoy me. Sometimes this annoyed me badly enough that I got busy being annoyed and I completely lost the point of my training that day. These guys have no right to be telling me what I need to work on! Especially someone who's only been training that long!

Then one day a thought walked over and smacked me in the temple. If someone with that little experience can see how much I need to improve something, maybe I should be paying attention to it. It really doesn't matter how skilled they are. I can take what they say with openness and appreciation and gratitude. If they can see it, then there may be a very obvious weakness that I need to work on. The one thing I am hundred percent sure about my budo is that it's not perfect.

I also understand that not all advice offered by juniors is good. Sometimes I have to explore it. I'll ask, "What do you mean?" or "Why do you see that as a problem?" Then we can talk and explore their concern together, and if it's a valid point, I've got another item to add to my already long list of things to fix, or they learn why their understanding may not be as strong as they thought. Either way, we learn something.

If we are honest with ourselves, our budo becomes a search for improvement and not an ego-building exercise related to how much more we know than someone else. I've reached the point where I'll take help improving myself from anywhere I can get it. I'm a slow learner, so if I'm going to accomplish much of anything before I die,

I've got to take all the help and assistance I can get. Even if it's from my own students.

Recently, I've started doing something new. I ask my students to sit down. Then I demonstrate something. Their job is not to look at it and think about how they can emulate what their teacher is doing. Their job is to look at what a fellow traveler on the budo path is doing, and help him. I ask them to tell me about anything they see that I should correct. It's a lot of fun and we all learn something from it. The more senior students are quite capable of telling me in detail about a lot of things I should work on. Often these are the same points I've just finished bringing to their attention in their own practice. At first, it's embarrassing to have a student call you out for the same problem you were helping them with fifteen minutes before. I had to work at not being embarrassed by this and just accepting their help. If I've just pointed something out to them, they are hyperaware of it, so if I'm off by one degree, they see it.

After a few run-throughs though, I've gotten past most of my ego issues (if I ever transcend them all, you're invited to my investiture as a living Buddha). At first, my goal was to take advantage of my senior student's ability and knowledge to help improve my practice. Now I've begun to see some other benefits. All my students gain from this. They really focus on trying to see more clearly in my practice what I have been asking them to do in theirs. Even the novice students begin to see better because they are looking for things at higher levels and advancing their understanding based on what other students are saying and what I am doing.

Once I fold up my ego, put it in a bag, stomp it thoroughly flat, and kick it to the back of the closet, we all win. I get progressively better and more subtle critiques from my own students. In turn, they become more discriminating about their own practice. They begin to understand what they are trying to achieve, and they can see where they want to go. Then we can work together to get there. We all advance.

That's the spirit of learning that I love to see in the *dojo*. We are all there trying to improve. Ultimately, there is no perfection in budo. There is only progress. Once I put aside my ego, I know I can learn from everyone. Now I'm teaching my students how to critique me so I can improve at the same time they are learning to see with clearer understanding what some of the goals of practice are. Enter the *dojo* in the spirit of learning, and you can learn from anyone, not just the people you address as "*Sensei.*"

TRAINING HARD AND TRAINING WELL ARE NOT THE SAME THING

We want to get the most out of our training. We look up to people who train hard and constantly push themselves. It seems obvious that the harder you train the better you will be. In judo, we respect the people who train harder, with more intensity than anyone else. All that sweat dripping on the mat has to mean something, doesn't it?

I was practicing piano, and one of my weaknesses there struck me as identical to problems most of us have in the *dojo* practicing budo. All practice is not equal. Some kinds of practice give far superior returns on the time and effort invested than other types of training. Poor training habits and techniques waste time. Worse, they can lead to ingraining bad habits and techniques that actually make us worse at what we are studying than we were before the training

I was practicing some *études* (French for, get this, *kata)* that are fundamental exercises for training the fingers on the piano. These are the boring exercises everyone rushes through so they can get to the good stuff—the real music, the real budo. Music études are like *kihon waza* practice in budo. These are the fundamental movements that you have to practice beyond the ability to do them properly, beyond the ability to do them properly without thinking about them, to the point where you can't do them incorrectly.

The tricky part is practicing them correctly in the first place so you don't develop bad habits that slow you down later. The first, most common, and biggest mistake with *études* and *kihon waza* is to treat them as mindless, boring exercises. These exercises teach your body and mind the most critical foundations of everything else you will do. If you try to rush them, or try to avoid thinking about them by thinking about your laundry or your job or your friends while doing them, you will likely be doing them wrong, and drilling this wrongness into your bones.

To do basics correctly as a beginner, you have to think about how you are doing them. When you have stopped being a beginner, you probably don't have to think about the basics when you are doing more advanced things, but when you are practicing the basics, you still need to think about them. If you don't, you risk letting mistakes and poor technique slip in. You also miss all the benefits that come from mindful practice. Be aware of what you're doing. As you are practicing basic techniques, look for things that can be improved. In a hundred repetitions, you'll be lucky if you have ten that you love. You'll also be lucky if you only have ten that you hate. The rest will be somewhere in between. The goal is to be aware of every repetition and to try and drag your worst reps up to the quality of your mediocre ones, and the mediocre reps up to the level of the best. Like all of budo, this is a never ending activity, since as soon as you improve, you'll start trying to reach a higher level.

Another pitfall on the practice path is rushing. If you've ever heard a young (or in my case, not so young) musician rush through a section of a piece, you've heard how wrong rushing can be. Don't rush your practice, even if you don't have much time. Rushing through things is worse than not practicing. If you don't practice, you don't improve, but you also don't pick up bad habits. If you rush something, you are doing it at the wrong speed, which is just wrong. If you don't have a lot of time, just do what you have time to do properly. When you rush, correct form is only the first thing that is lost.

You also sacrifice the rhythm and feel of proper technique, and you lose the awareness of what you are doing. In this sort of situation, your training can only move backward as you reinforce bad form, bad timing, and poor thought.

One of the most popular parts of judo practice is also one of judo practice's biggest weaknesses. *Randori*, or judo style sparring, is fun, so much fun that often students would rather do this than work on their basics. There are lot of things that can go wrong with *randori* though. The first problem is all that fun. We are all susceptible to this one. It's easy to spend all our time doing the fun parts of training, whatever it is, and neglect the parts that don't grab our attention and gratify our hearts. This is true in all arts, even in *koryu* budo where there is very little sparring type practice. There are some *kata* that are just more interesting, and others that frustrate me until I am ready to scream because I just never seem to get them right.

One particular form this trap takes is practicing what we are good at. We enjoy practicing things we are good at much more than the parts that we haven't mastered yet. I love doing Harai Goshi and Tai Otoshi in judo because I do them better than anything else. That's exactly why I should limit my practice of them though. The fact that I can do them better than anything else should tell me how much more I need to be practicing everything else. Spend most of your time practicing what you aren't good at. That's where you'll improve the most.

The second problem with *randori* and other sparring practices is the tendency for people to go faster and faster as the *randori* session continues. *Randori* is a form of practice, not a competition to see who is better. People usually forget this point within ten seconds of the start of a session. As soon as you stop thinking about *randori* or sparring as practice and start treating it as another sort of competition, it's practice value plummets. You stop trying your weaker techniques that you should be polishing, and switch to your favorite techniques. People also start getting defensive because they don't want to lose. In judo, this means all sorts of bad postures and muscling to prevent throws. Instead, they should be working on ingraining good posture and movement, which will allow them to execute good, effective technique.

The third problem I see is that people don't go into *randori* with a plan to use it to get better. Go into a *randori* session with a plan for what you want to practice and improve. Don't worry about winning and losing. It's practice, so you're getting better is what constitutes winning, not beating the other guy. If all you do is worry about winning, you've already lost the chance to improve, and worse, you're likely to pick up bad habits in the effort to win. Pick a technique you need to work on and focus on finding where that technique fits in the movement. Or just work on how you move and sense your partner. Take the time to develop an understanding of how people move and react. These sorts of practices will make your budo much better, polish your skills, and improve your fundamentals.

Pick a speed and intensity for your practice that suits the points you want to work on. Slow is great for some things. Fast and light might work better for polishing something like foot sweeps. Think about what you want to get out of a *randori* or sparring session and how you will have to train to get that. Don't just rush in and throw everything you are working on to the floor.

When you go all out to win during practice, the best you can hope for is that you win without developing any bad habits. You don't get any better. The worst that can happen is that you develop and ingrain bad habits from trying to win and not lose, while developing a counterproductive attitude about winning and losing.

Training at less than 100 percent intensity is tough, because we associate training hard with effective training. This is true when you are working on cardio or strength development. You only improve your physical condition when you push the limits of what you can do. The more you sweat, the harder you work, the stronger you get and the more your stamina increases.

When you are working on technique however, hard training gets in the way of good training and can turn into bad training. Adding muscle, as I keep rediscovering, does not improve technique. Oddly though, adding technical skill does make muscle more effective. Interesting how that works. In order to make your physical strength as useful and effective as possible, you have to work at practicing without it. Once the technique is smooth and fluid, then you can try adding a little speed and strength *at the proper moment for those to be useful.* Strength and speed are not always benefits. Using them at the wrong time is a waste of energy and can destroy the effectiveness of a technique. I have lots experience at finding ways to blow a perfectly good technique, and adding strength or speed at the wrong moment is one of the surest.

There's one other area where the temptation to practice too hard is too frequently succumbed to. That's when practicing "real" techniques, such as self-defense techniques. The allure of doing the technique as hard and as fast as we can because this is for self-defense and we want to be sure it will work is a powerful one. It's even more irresistible than my wife's cookies fresh out of the oven on the cooling rack when she's left the room. The problem with this is the same as in *randori* and sparring. We can start relying on bad techniques and too much muscle and speed to get by. This is fine until you run into someone with good technique, or even just someone faster or stronger.

A better method is to practice the technique at a very low intensity. As you get more comfortable at it, have your partner increase the intensity slightly. When you can do the technique calmly and smoothly at the new intensity, have your partner step it up again. Eventually you'll be able to do the technique calmly and smoothly with your partner attacking as intensely as they can. You'll have good technique, and you'll be accustomed to maintaining calm and relaxed, effective technique even under intense, strong attacks. If you jump straight into working at high-intensity levels it will take much longer to master the technique, if you ever do. More likely you will develop bad habits to compensate for the skill you don't have yet, which will just make developing the skill that much more difficult.

Train slow and work up to it. It's easy to practice things incorrectly. The temptation is always there to start practicing harder, faster, and more intensely than your technique is ready for. Don't give in. Practice right so you truly learn how to do the techniques and master your art.

This site has a very nice article about practicing from a musical perspective: http://www.musicforbrass.com/articles/art-of-practicing.html

WHEN IT COMES TO TRAINING, FAST IS SLOW AND SLOW IS FAST

In the previous section, I was talking about the mistakes people make in practicing, and it appears I gave the impression that I think that hard training is always wrong. After rereading what I wrote, I can see how that happened. I spent most of the article talking about the problems with hard training, and only the bit that I repeat below about how to train hard properly.

Train slow and work up to it. It's easy to practice things incorrectly. The temptation is always there to start practicing harder, faster, and more intensely than your technique is ready for. Don't give in. Practice right so you truly learn how to do the techniques and master your art.

There is an old saying in martial arts circles that "fast is slow, and slow is fast." The most vivid example I've seen of this was when I was watching my iaido teacher, Suda *Sensei*, do kendo with high school students. At the time, Suda *Sensei* was eighty years old. He didn't have the raw speed or strength or stamina that these sixteen-to eighteen-year-old kids did. If all it took was physical speed and strength, they would have blown him right out of the *dojo*. Instead, he totally dominated them while seeming to move in slow motion when compared to his young opponents. These are not just strong kids either. A lot of these kids had been doing kendo for ten years or longer, so they were pretty good technically too.

Still, they would march out on the floor, and these strong, young guys wouldn't be able to do anything against him. It wasn't that *Sensei* was faster and stronger and crushed them. He was simply always where he should be. You never saw him take advantage of an opening. That would have required speed. Instead, his *shinai* was there filling the spot as the opening came into existence. He was slow, and he moved slowly (at least compared to eighteen-year-old high-school athletes who train every day). He never rushed, and he never hurried. He understood how his partner was moving, and he put his sword just in the right place at the right time to make a beautiful cut. He didn't have to hurry. He could move slowly because more importantly than being fast or strong, he knew how to move and where to be and always did it correctly.

You don't achieve that kind of understanding, control, and soft, effortless movement by spending all your time training hard. You get there by training right. Training right means not training any harder than you can while still supporting correct posture, breathing, and movement. This is the tricky part. You do need to train as hard as you can while doing everything correctly. If you are training so hard, and going so fast that you can't maintain correct posture, correct movement, correct breathing, and correct technique, then you are training too hard. The biggest problem with this is that you then teach yourself bad posture, poor movement, lousy, shallow breathing, and weak technique.

The trick is to push yourself right up to that edge where everything starts to fall apart, but not fall over it. It's easy to go too far, and I still find myself doing it from time to time. Try as I might to eliminate it, I still have some ego about this stuff, and sometimes it gets the best of me. I rely on my friends and seniors to help me avoid this, and to stop me when I start crossing the line into bad training.

One of the first keys to training as hard as you can properly, is to start slow. That whole "slow is fast, and fast is slow" thing starts here. If you try to rush your training, you will improve slowly, if at all, because you will be training in bad technique, poor posture, incorrect movement, and shallow, inefficient breathing. Start slow, well below your best speed and your highest effective intensity level. Whatever it is you are practicing, focus and do it perfectly. Then increase the intensity. Not the strength or the speed. Just the intensity. Increase your focus, blast everything else out of your mind except what you are doing and doing 100 percent. Gradually increase the speed, but never so much that you lose control.

If you've got a partner, controlling this sort of thing is much easier. It's one of the reasons that *koryu* budo *ryuha* require lower level students to always work with a senior student who will act as the *uke* for the technique or the *kata*. The senior student initiates the interaction and sets the speed and intensity level. The goal is to always set it just above where the student is comfortable, but below the point where their technique and control fall apart. That is a pretty narrow range for most us. I know that my technique starts to break down fairly soon after we move out of my comfort zone.

The goal is to expand that comfort zone, to make you able to handle more and more stress without getting tense, breathing shallowly, pulling your shoulders up by your ears, and rocking back on your heels. Good teachers and seniors will feel where a training partner is at and adjust the training appropriately. You want to spend plenty of time training out in that shadowy region where you aren't comfortable but you still have enough control to move properly, maintain good posture, breathe well, and execute good technique. This is where you will make the most progress.

Each time you train there, you will stretch your comfort zone a little further out, and the point where technique, posture, breathing, and movement all fall apart will move a little further away as well. This isn't necessarily hard training as we are used to thinking about it. It is hard though, and it will leave you dripping in sweat from the focus, concentration, and control required for training out there in the shadowland between comfort and losing control. It takes a long time to learn how to push yourself far enough but not too far.

I think this is why *koryu* students seem, in my experience, to make more rapid progress than students of modern arts. It's not that *koryu* curricula are inherently better. The *koryu* training system is much better though. Beginners and lower level students always train with a senior, whose job is to keep them training out past their comfort zone without going too far. The student doesn't have to worry about how hard or intensely to train. The senior sets the pace and makes sure the training is fast and hard, but not too fast or too hard. This way the students get the maximum benefit from their time in the *dojo*.

A problem I see with many modern budo is that people spend a lot of time doing repetitions on their own, without enough supervision to make sure that what they are doing are high-quality repetitions that train good techniques into their muscles. Then the students are encouraged to spar and do *randori* with people of all levels, without any control as to how hard they are fighting. Students push themselves too hard, worry about winning (or not losing), and teach themselves bad habits that they will be trying to undo for decades. (Trust me, I have this little bend at the waist in Harai Goshi

I have been fighting for close to twenty-five years. And I won't even mention how quickly I can fall into a bad defensive posture. Argh!)

Don't rush into training harder than you are ready for. Also don't rush into trying to learn techniques and *kata* before you are ready for them. Doing that does two things. It waters down the amount of time you have to develop each technique because you are chasing too many skills at the same time. On top of that, it makes it more difficult for your body to absorb any of the skills effectively because you are trying to absorb more than you are capable of absorbing. The result is that you are studying more stuff but learning it more slowly. Fast is slow and slow is fast.

Learn the most basic things really solidly before you add more stuff to it. I know well the desire to learn the advanced techniques. The secret is that there are no advanced techniques. There are only the basics applied so well that they seem advanced. Hiroshi Ikeda *Sensei* once said, "We teach all the secrets of aikido in the first class." It's true. On the first day, you learn about relaxing, moving properly, and breathing. Learn the basics well and all your techniques will look like magic. I was at a seminar where Howard Popkin kept doing impossible things to me. He used no advanced techniques, nothing complicated. He performed very basic techniques and applications so smoothly and effectively that they felt like magic. And you know what? Even those of us doing them for the very first time could do the techniques effectively when we slowed down so we could do the movements properly. The moment we tried to speed things up though, everything fell apart. There is no way to learn the good stuff by rushing. You have to slow down and do it right. Fast is slow and slow is fast.

Learn good, powerful budo. Learn techniques that are so smooth and effective people accuse of you doing magic and tell you they can't imagine being able to do what you do. Master your body and your technique so fully that you fill every opening your partner gives you before it has opened. Be so relaxed and move so slowly while completely dominating your opponents that people watching can't understand how you do it. The fastest way to get there is to slow down and go no faster than you can do the technique correctly. Fast is slow and slow is fast.

GETTING OUT OF THE COMFORT ZONE

We like training. It's fun. We value it. Training is good for us. That's why we do it. We like what we are doing and what it does for us. All those benefits that budo training is supposed to give are great, right? Budo is great training for the body, all that exercise and developing speed and agility and strength. Then there are those mental benefits of being calm and centered and confident and mentally resilient.

Except when we aren't actually getting most of these benefits. It's easy to train and not really progress. I know there have been periods where I went to judo and did the whole workout but never really progressed or improved in any of the areas I just listed. Yes, it was a good workout and I maintained my level of fitness. Yes, the exercise felt great. Yes, I did a lot of techniques, but they were all techniques I already had a reasonable level of mastery of. Yes, I had to focus and work my mind but it, was more of a reinforcement and repetition of lessons learned. I knew what I could do, and I did it. What I didn't do was more. I didn't push my body to its limits of strength. I certainly didn't do anything that made me develop my speed or agility. When it came to mental training, I did things I was already confident that I could do. It's easy to be calm and centered when you're working well within your comfort zone.

None of this is really training. It's more like maintenance. It's just keeping up with what has been achieved in the past. It doesn't improve me in any way though. In truth, even when I'm doing those things, I'm diminishing. When I don't test my limits, they start shrinking because I'm not sure where they are. If I'm not out close to the edge, I lose sight of where it is and my imagination always makes it closer than it really is. When I'm not sure where the edge is, I naturally give myself a plentiful safety zone so I don't accidentally stray across the edge into uncertain territory.

I will admit that there are times in life when just treading water is tough enough. Most of the time though, we can do better. The question is, how do we know we're doing better? A simple clue is your answer to the question "Am I in my comfort zone?" If you answer yes to this question, you're not getting any better. If you're not in your comfort zone, even if you're just a little bit outside it, you're pushing your limits and growing.

Ultimately, I'm responsible for the progress of my training. I have to push myself and find people to help me advance each step along the road. In judo, if I just show up every week and do my stuff, no one will say anything, and people will be happy that I'm participating. If I want to really learn, they'll be thrilled. It's my choice and my responsibility. We each have to work at pushing our limits.

For most of us, the first time we set foot in the *dojo*, we are pushing against more limits than we realize. We are learning to master our bodies and our minds. We are learning about power and conflict dynamics in the most fundamental way, by actually learning to fight. We are learning to go beyond the raw physical conflict and master our minds and ourselves. Often, we are pushing limits society has told us we can't go beyond, that we can't be good at dealing with violence because good people don't do that. It can be difficult enough if you're male. I can't imagine the pressure against that first step if you're female.

Once we've taken that first step and trained for a while, the new danger is complacency. After we achieve a certain degree of competency at budo, or anything, the danger is leaning back, letting out a big sigh, and thinking, "I'm good." At that moment, we're in danger of stopping dead in the path and not learning anything new. This is true of anything we do, not just budo.

In a lot of things in life, a certain level of competency is sufficient. One of the wonders of budo is that there is no such thing as good enough. I have been privileged to train with people in their eighties and nineties who were, and are, striving to improve. They still get out in the *dojo* and actively work at becoming better today than they were yesterday. It's inspiring to see something people like this. Hada Hidetoshi was ninety-one when he passed his sixth *dan* in iaido on November 19, 2013.

The key to this is to keep searching for that edge. If you're outside your comfort zone, even just a little, you're growing. So how do you know where that edge is? Well, first, are you at all uncomfortable? For many years, I had the good fortune to train with a wonderful man, Hikoso *Sensei*, in Shiga, Japan. The last twenty minutes of each training session was left for *randori*. I always ran and grabbed *Sensei* because he was so good I couldn't do anything to him, while he could toss me any time he wanted. I learned from every three-minute session he gave me. I noticed after a while though that most of the time no one asked him to do *randori*. In fact, people went out of their way to avoid meeting his eyes and getting asked to play. (And yes, it was play. He always had the biggest smile through the whole session. It was pure fun for him.)[1]

---

1   The results of the 1993 6th dan test for iaido in Toyko, Japan can be found at http:// www.kendo.or.jp/examination/iaido-6dan/20131116-tokyo/result/.

I finally asked some people why they never trained with him, and they all told me, "He's too good." They didn't want to train with someone they felt they had no chance of throwing. They didn't want to go out of their comfort zone. On the other hand, that was exactly why I loved training with him. For me, it was a personal victory when I progressed enough to be able to break his balance a little. I wasn't near to throwing him, but I had become good enough to affect him. Yes, I knew I wasn't going to throw him. Yes, I knew he would throw me. It was exciting, and I really had to work and present my very best judo just to stay standing.

Over time though, my comfort zone increased. Practicing with Hikoso *Sensei* made everyone else much less intimidating. After *Sensei* had thrown me around, even the big, tough guys didn't seem nearly as imposing. And then one day a miracle happened. I'd been working on a technique, with *Sensei* in mind, I admit, and one day the universe aligned in my favor and I THREW *Sensei*. He was laughing in joy and excitement before he hit the mat. He was as thrilled that I had progressed far enough to throw him as I was. When he got up, he made a bow to me with a grand smile, and then we came together and continued the *randori* session. It was fabulous.

If I had, like some many others in the *dojo*, stayed in my comfort zone and only trained with people I was already able to throw from time to time, I would never have progressed to the level where I could throw Hikoso *Sensei*.

You have to go out past the edge of your comfort zone. That's the only way it will get bigger. If you look at a training partner and think, "There's no way I can do anything to him," then you're probably outside your comfort zone.

If training with someone makes your heart beat a little faster and your breathing pick up, that's another good sign. When I do jodo or *kenjutsu*, there are certain partners who I know will be coming in faster and harder than I'm used to. I trust them to not hurt me, but still, I know I'm out on the edge of my ability to keep up, and I may not be able to get out of the way in time or get the block up or place the counterattack properly to stop them. It's thrilling. I know I'm learning when I train with them. They push me to improve every time we meet.

Another clue is your mind. Are you worried about making mistakes? Are you concerned that you could fail to do things right? These are clues that you are in the right zone. If you don't have questions about your ability to do something, you're not pushing your limits. If you're not concerned about completely blowing the movement or getting overwhelmed in *randori*, you're not advancing. If you are putting yourself out there and making the mistakes, being overwhelmed by your training partner, then you're pushing on down the path, and your comfort zone is expanding.

Don't stay where you are. Budo is a path, not a seat. Don't give in to the temptation to sit down and stay where you are. There is always more to be learned, another hill to go round, and another river to cross. Push yourself. Take the losses. Make the mistakes. Go where you can't win. It doesn't always feel like it, but when you push your limits, you are progressing, and that development can show up when no one is expecting it. I was barely dreaming of it, and I know Hikoshiso *Sensei* wasn't expecting it. One day though, everything I had learned about sensing and responding to movement that I had gleaned from hours of frustrating practice when it felt like I was fighting a mountain came together, and suddenly *Sensei* was airborne. And laughing all the way to the ground because I had learned enough out there on the edge that I could catch him in a bad movement.

THERE ARE NO ADVANCED TECHNIQUES

There are no advanced techniques. Really. Early in my budo career, I was looking for the secret techniques and mysterious skills that would make me able to do the things my teachers did that seemed like magic. But what looks like magic is really just the basics done phenomenally well. It was hard to convince myself that Kano Jigoro's famous answer to the question "What is the secret of judo?" was entirely truthful. When asked about the secret of judo, Kano replied simply, "Practice, practice, practice." This is not an inspiring answer for a kid who wants to be able to effortlessly throw people across the room.

Sadly, for all of us who are seeking the magic, it seems to be true. Whether I'm working on judo or *kenjutsu* or iai or jo or my current nemesis, *kusarigama*, careful, considered, focused, and aware practice seems to be the real secret. More and more often, my own students look at something I've done with them like it's impossible, which is something I fondly remember thinking about my own teachers. It's a reaction I never have any more though. Even when I can't begin to do what my teachers are doing, I can see how they are doing it and I can see the path to being able to do it myself.

Last week, I was working on some *taijutsu* with an aikido teacher and friend. Jim can do incredible things to your balance and make you fall down with the subtlest of movements. It's a very different technique than what I do in judo, but I can feel what he's doing. The principle of what he does is clear. He is taking my balance (in judo, we call this *kuzushi*) and then drawing me in a direction where

I can't support myself. I have to fall down. What makes it magic is that Jim does this with the least amount of movement possible. My judo techniques have long been built on very large movements, but the principle is the same. Now I'm working on bringing a little bit of Jim's magic into my judo.

It won't happen with mindless repetitions of techniques though. You can repeat a technique as often as you like, and you won't learn anything from the repetitions or get any better. You have to be fully engaged in your practice and mentally looking for slight differences in your technique that will make you better. That's practice. Just doing something a hundred or a thousand times won't make you better. It will make whatever you are doing more solidly anchored in your body. If you are repeating poor technique, it will make it that much more difficult to change and improve your technique.

To get better at Jim's throws from a wrist grab, I didn't repeat what I already knew. I didn't repeat the big movement judo techniques that I have been doing. I slowed down and focused on exactly what was happening to my partner when I moved just a little bit. I focused on feeling exactly when my partner's balance shifted from being supported by his frame to relying on me to keep from falling over. It was just a tiny bit of weight that was transferred to me, so little that I doubt my partner even realized he was using me to stay up. Once that happened though, all I had to do was turn my wrist over and he fell down, because I was withdrawing my support of his body. Jim can do this at full speed. It takes me several slow seconds to do it. By being aware of what is going on and practicing it slowly, I can develop the sensitivity to do this faster and faster over time.

One of the keys to making this work is to know what I'm looking for and then focusing on developing that skill and sensitivity. If we just go to the *dojo* and quickly repeat the techniques we already know, we won't improve much. We have to be willing to slow down enough that we can focus on making changes to our technique. That's when practice really begins.

Up until last February, I had what is a fairly strong Hiki Otoshi Uchi strike in Shinto Muso Ryu. Then I had the chance to train with one of the senior teachers in our group. I was lucky enough to watch him correcting a junior and demonstrate his technique over and over for my fellow student. What a fantastic opportunity for me! As I watched, I could see small differences between how he was swinging the *jo* and meeting the sword and the way I was doing the technique.

The technique is the same one I've been working on for years. There is no magic here, just a more subtle, smoother use of the *jo* that results in a powerful, inexorable technique requiring far less effort than what I've been doing. It's up to me to increase my understanding of this fundamental technique that I started learning on my first day of practice. It's not magic. It's not a special, advanced technique taught only to senior students. It's simply a fundamental technique done really, really well.

This is true of everything I have done in budo. When I wrote about Hikkoso *Sensei* tossing me around the judo mat by waving his hands, I wasn't referring to any special, advanced technique. What he does is an extremely effective application of the basic principle of *kuzushi*. What Hikkoso *Sensei* did to me is very similar to what I'm beginning to understand in my friend Jim's technique, and both are extensions of the first principle of technique in judo, which has been referenced in every judo practice I've ever attended in any of many different countries. It's not a secret. Hikkoso *Sensei* and Jim are just applying a basic principle extremely well. The same goes for that Shinto Muso Ryu teacher. He wasn't doing anything secret or arcane. He was doing the third technique taught in Shinto Muso Ryu amazingly well.

None of these people have any secrets. In truth, they are doing exactly the opposite of keeping secrets. They put what they have learned through practice out there for students and fellow *budoka* to see and learn from. One of the first steps is to stop thinking of it as secret magic and start thinking of it as an attainable skill. Then it's really all about the quality and quantity of your practice. It's easy to wish that Kano *Sensei*'s secret had been something besides "practice, practice, practice."

There aren't any special techniques only taught to advanced students. We keep practicing, and step by step, the advanced techniques appear. Except that they aren't advanced techniques. They are the basics done so well they seem advanced.

ESSENTIALS

The various forms of budo are all human activities. They all deal with the most straightforward forms of conflict. They appear very different though. Judo, kendo, naginata, jodo, karatedo, iaido, kyudo. These are just a few of the forms that budo takes. Can there be anything essential across all of these disparate arts based in everything from empty hand strikes to short weapons to grappling to ranged weapons? I think there are at least three things which are essential to all budo forms: structure, spacing, and timing. These sections are each about one of these essential aspects of budo.

Figure 4: Daito Ryu demonstration at Kashima Shrine.
Photo copyright Grigoris Miliaresis 2014

THE MOST ESSENTIAL PRINCIPLES IN BUDO: STRUCTURE

A question came up in a budo group I'm part of, asking what the three most important concepts in budo are. It's an interesting question. What ideas are most fundamental in the art you practice? These concepts undergird and direct your training. They direct the focus of your training and what sort of things you are practicing. People offered quite a few ideas.

Keep your body relaxed.

Always keep your center (or be centered).

Keep your elbows down, and close to your body.

Always try to control the first move.

Many of the ideas offered were specific to aikido, which is the point of that group. My thoughts are more general and apply to any form of budo. My list is structure/stance, spacing, and timing, in that order. Each builds on where the previous concept is, and without effective use of the previous concept the next cannot be employed effectively. All apply regardless of whether you are doing kung fu, judo, boxing, aikido, swords, staves, or scary stuff like *kusarigama*. This is my list, and I make no claim that it is definitive. I offer it in the hope of sparking good conversation and consideration of the most important elements of practice and application. I'd thought to do these all in one section, but it looks like it's I'm going to have to give each one its own section.

My first principle is structure/stance. Without a solid, connected, supported structure, you can't accomplish anything. This why I'm only partly joking when I say that <u>the only thing I really teach is how to walk and how to breathe.</u> Good structure is what allows the fastest, most effective, stable, and strong movement. If you are slouching and rolling your shoulders, tipping your head at the ground and not supporting yourself, you can't breathe deeply or efficiently. Slouching and poor posture compress the torso so it cannot hold as much air. You will get tired more quickly just because you can't get enough oxygen into your body fast enough.

Slouching also robs the body of its natural structural integrity. If you slouch, you're off-balance already. Judo folks stand or fall based on their balance, but this is true for anyone in any art. If you're not balanced, you're not stable in at least one direction.

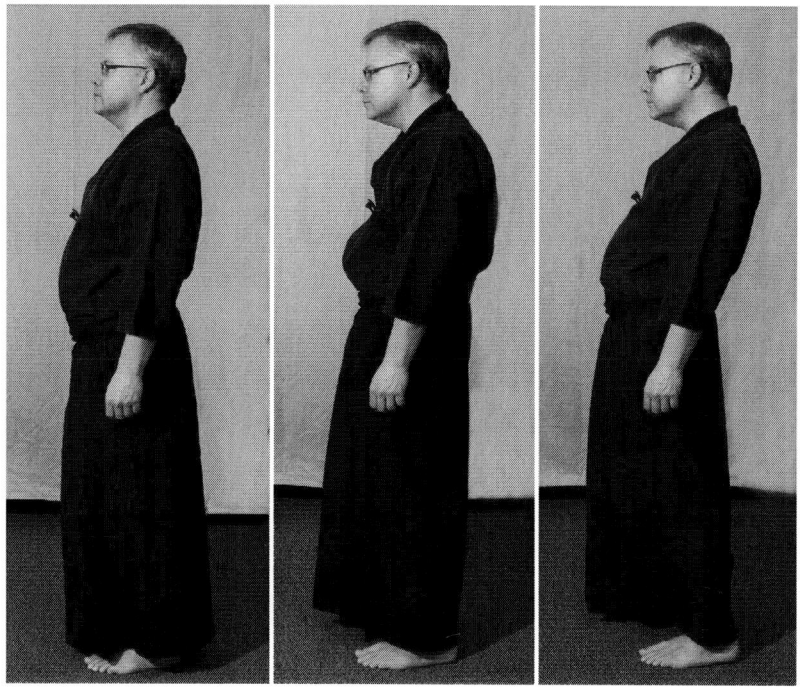

Figure 5: Good posture, Slouching forward, Slumping back Photo copyright Rick Frye, 2016

In the picture above the two diagrams on the right show what our structure looks like when we slouch. Can you imagine trying to do any physical activity with that sort of compromised structure?

With good structure, loads and forces can easily be absorbed and handled; movement is quick, light, and easy; and changes can be adapted to readily. Without it, we can't carry or absorb loads or force; movement is difficult, slow, and tiring; and it is difficult to adapt to changes in the situation.

I've been showing this to my sword and *jo* students for years with a simple exercise. I let them hold a *jo* against my solar plexus in whatever way they like holding the *jo*, and I can push the *jo* back into them and them across the room without any effort at all. They can't do a thing to slow me down and I can reach them with a weapon or my hands before they can do anything about it. If the structure of the wrist is off its optimal angle even a little, it will collapse under pressure and be useless.

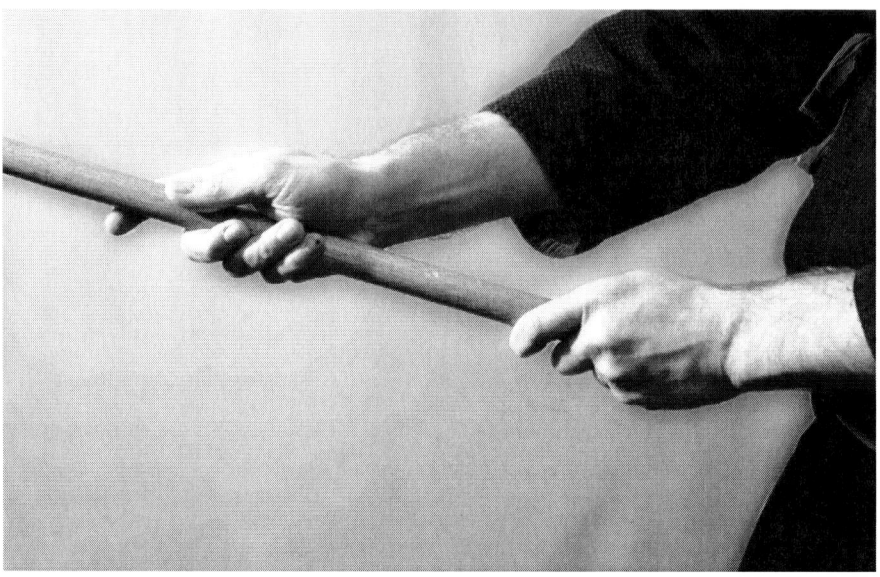

Figure 6; Left wrist structure is compromised. Photo copyright Rick Frye, 2017

On the other hand, if the wrist is at the proper angle, I can stick a 140-kg goon on the other end of the stick and he can't push into me, or even into someone half my size. How can it be that just changing the angle of the wrist where you hold the stick can have such an impact? I'll let the mechanical engineers and the physics boys explain the details because I don't have a deep enough background there to do it anything like accurate justice.

Figure 7: Left wrist shows strong structure. Photo copyright Rick Frye, 2017

There is a split between weak structural configurations and strong ones carries over to every joint in the body and to the way the body as a whole is arranged. If the wrist structure is good but another joint such as the hip, knee, or ankle is not aligned properly, the whole body structure is still weak and will collapse even if pressured only slightly.

Structure gives the body the ability to move, and when that structure is taken away, there isn't much anyone can do. At a seminar, Howard Popkin impressed that upon me anew. He can, by simply moving around the force and structure of the body, completely undermine the power of people bigger and stronger than I am and throw them casually, without so much as taking a deep breath. He simply maintained his structure and went around the lines of strength in mine.

You can push all you want on someone who keeps their structure aligned so your force is directed into the floor. It takes very little strength to maintain your structure under this kind of attack. The attacker's force actually pushes your body to maintain good structure without the addition of much energy on your part. If you decide to push back, it's easy to do so because your structure is already supporting and negating their power. When you push back, they fly.

It's interesting that according to Kano Jigoro, founder of Kodokan Judo, one of the two great secrets of great judo is *kuzushi* (崩し). *Kuzushi* comes from a verb in Japanese that means tearing down, knocking down, or breaking things into smaller parts. Sometimes, it implies undermining and destroying a foundation. This is one of the great realizations of Kano's that he put into his judo. If you destroy the foundation of someone's structure, take them off their foundation, and remove the support from their structure; they become incredibly weak and a small woman can throw a large man.

This is true for whatever art you are practicing, whether it is armed or unarmed, jujutsu, karate, sword or chain, and staff or rope. You maintain your posture and then you destroy your opponent's.

The first step in mastering budo is learning to properly maintain your own structure. If you can't do that, nothing else is possible. Once you've got that, you have a powerful base to work from. Then you learn to manipulate and undermine your opponent's structure. Once you destroy the integrity of their structure, throws and joint locks are easy. The key is that destroying the integrity of someone's structure doesn't involve harming them. It just means making them slump or slouch or come away from a balanced stance. Once you've done that, the actual technique isn't terribly important because without a solid, balanced structure, it's nearly impossible to defend oneself, even from a very poor attack.

Judoka spend an immense amount of time practicing off-balancing techniques to accomplish this. Aikido folks work on movements to draw someone out of good physical alignment. Daito Ryu folks work on doing it with the smallest movements possible. It all comes down to the same thing. Destroy the ability of the body's structure to support it, and the person can't resist anything.

There are the two sides of structure in budo. Create and maintain a solid, efficient, mobile structure in yourself while undermining your opponent's structure and making it unable to support him and his movements. Mastery of structure is absolutely essential to everything we do in budo. We can't begin to move and breathe properly until we learn to do so with good structure. We can't defend against anything without good structure. Effective attacks are impossible with an unstable structure.

Good structure is at the root of all good budo, whether it is a striking art, a grappling art, or a weapons art. Without good structure, you have nothing. That's why it's the first of my essential principles of budo.

THE MOST ESSENTIAL PRINCIPLES IN BUDO: SPACING

There is no single essential element of good budo. There are a number of elements that make up the common foundations of all good budo, whether it is with empty hands, small weapons, swords, spears, and *naginata* or even in *kyubado*. I wrote about structure previously. Another essential principle is *ma'ai* (間合), often translated as spacing. This one seems simple, and turns out to be exceedingly complex and subtle.

At its most basic level, spacing is the distance between you and your opponent. That's the most basic level. After this, it quickly gets complicated. *Ma'ai* (間合) is a Japanese term, and while it refers to distance, it also implies the *proper* or *correct* distance. The problem and complexity comes from the fact that what is the proper distance is different for every encounter.

Let's start just with empty hand encounters to keep it simple. I'm 183 cm tall. My reach and range is longer than someone who is 160 cm tall, assuming we're both using the same sorts of attacks. My range is longer, so I don't need to be as close to reach out, make a connection, and apply a judo technique. An opponent who is 160 cm has to come well within my range before she can attack.

Seems simple enough. How about this then? I'm a *judoka*, so I'm not big with punches and kicks. So let's assume my 160 cm opponent is now proficient at tae kwon do. Oops! The *ma'ai* just changed significantly, and not in my favor. Now my opponent's kicks are effective at a greater range than my grappling. On the other hand, if I get inside her effective range, my grappling is more effective than her striking.

So good distancing, *maʾai*, changes with the person's reach and the techniques being used. It's the combination of your effective attacking range and your opponent's. What's good for one is more than likely not optimal for the other. Kendo breaks down *maʾai* into several discrete ranges, which is easier in kendo because the length of the *shinai* is controlled to prevent major differences between *kendoka*. The kendo community has analyzed their three main ranges, *toma*, *issoku-no-maʾai*, and *chika-ma* (outside of attack range, attack with one step, close enough to attack without moving). Their analysis is focused on two very similar opponents with identical weapons.

Once we get outside the competitive arena with its requirement that things be "fair," whatever that might be, *maʾai* becomes a very fluid distance. In both *gendai* and *koryu* arts, *kata* are designed to teach the fluidity of *maʾai* by setting up the student to practice against a variety of weapons and partners. This is true in judo in the Kime No *kata* where the student must deal with everything from grabs to strikes to knife attacks to swords. It's true in most aikido training as well, with a variety of *tanto* and sword disarms.

Many classical bujutsu systems cover the entire gamut of weapons combinations, from both persons unarmed to one person armed, to both armed with the same weapon to asymmetrically armed training. Many weapons arts mostly emphasize asymmetrical training scenarios. In Shinto Muso Ryu, the only time both partners are armed alike is in a few of the *okuden* forms and seven of the Shinto Ryu *kenjutsu kata*. In Jikishinkage Ryu, the combination is usually sword versus *naginata*. Most *koryu* arts include a variety of weapons in their curriculum.

Once we get to this variety of combinations, the terms for *ma'ai* become much more interesting and challenging. If I'm holding a *kodachi* facing an opponent with a *tachi*, her *issoku-no-ma'ai* is longer than mine. If I switch to *jo*, mine is now longer than hers. If she's got one of those giant *naginata* or a *yari*, hers is longer than mine. And then we have the variability of some types of *kusarigama*, but I'm not going to go there for now.

The continually changing combination of an individual's range and her weapon's range makes *ma'ai* exceptionally difficult to master (and even more complicated to write about). By practicing with a variety of partners and in a variety of weapon combinations, you can develop a good sense of *ma'ai*. I'm starting to understand some aspects of it, but I have a long way to go.

One thing that is critical for learning *ma'ai* is that attacks have to be effective. I hear a lot about "sincere" and "committed" attacks in some arts. I'll be honest; I really don't care if the attack is sincere or not, and I really don't care if it's committed. I care about whether it will be effective. A sincere, committed attack that will never reach you is worthless for training because you will never learn at what range you are vulnerable and at what range you are effective. The same is true for an attack that purposely misses to either side. I can't learn how to deal with an attack that isn't effective.

The attack doesn't have to be fast and hard. It doesn't have to be heavily overcommitted. It does have to be on target. That's the key. On any number of occasions, I've told students to hit me. They've swung their weapons and I haven't moved because I haven't needed to. I could see they weren't doing anything that would impact me. I stood there and watched their weapons swing past in the breeze. Then people asked why I didn't move. I didn't move because my sense of *ma'ai* is strong enough that I can see when someone is attacking effectively and when he is just waving at empty air. Waving at empty air is not effective or threatening.

Every attack, no matter how slow, has to be such that it would impact my position. If it's not going to do that, how am I going to learn what distance and attack is dangerous and what isn't? If you don't know the difference, you will fall for every feint and false attack. An effective attack is not one where you overcommit and throw yourself at your opponent either. For an effective attack, you move in maintaining your balance and integrity while striking or cutting so that you will impact your partner if she doesn't move.

As you practice *kata* and *randori* with a variety of partners and weapons combinations, you will develop a more and more sensitive understanding of *ma'ai*. With an understanding of *ma'ai* comes awareness of the difference between an empty threat and a position that is vulnerable to attack. You will also be able to see when your opponent is open to attack on the other side. Without an understanding of *ma'ai*, you are vulnerable to every threat and intimidating move because you won't know the difference between an attack that will affect you and movement that cannot hurt you.

Note: "*Ma'ai*" has three syllables in Japanese: mah-ah-eye. In English, it comes out as two syllables: mah-eye.

THE MOST ESSENTIAL PRINCIPLES IN BUDO: TIMING

Earlier, I have written about structure and spacing. Closely related and entwined with spacing is timing. Timing is the subtle ingredient that makes spacing and structure appear to work like magic. If you have great structure and good control of the spacing, you're doing well and you can be quite effective. To be great though, you need to master timing.

Timing is what makes that incredible technique from Shinkage Ryu and other styles where the *tachi* cuts through the cutting sword of her opponent and into the opponent's head while driving the opponent's sword off the target into ineffective space. Too early and the opponent simply evades and counterattacks. Too late and the opponent's sword will slice right through you. There is a window of a fraction of a second in which to make this work. The same is true of the stop strike in Shinto Muso Ryu. Too early and the opponent easily evades. Too late and the cut will take off your arm before your attack can have any effect.

An entire class of techniques that requires perfect timing is judo foot sweeps like De Ashi Harai. When done correctly, the *uke* doesn't even notice the technique. They just notice the floor disappears from under their feet and then reappears between their shoulder blades. This technique, like the sword techniques, is deceptively simple. You merely sweep the foot of the *uke* to the side while they are walking. The trick lies in the fact that the foot has to be swept after the *uke* has transferred weight onto the foot but before the foot touches the ground. Timing here is everything. Too soon and there is no weight on the foot so sweeping has little effect. Too late and the foot is on the ground and solid, making the sweep impossible.

Timing is so important we don't often talk about it. We just practice things that require it without really focusing on how to see it. Good timing is something I'm still developing in my practice, so this is definitely a work in progress. For me, the first step in learning to understand and apply timing is recognizing that there are common elements that make certain moments optimal for action, and these common elements hold true whether it is an armed or unarmed art, whether you are at grappling distance, empty hand striking distance, long weapons distance, or even tangled with your opponent rolling on the floor.

A moment is optimal when an opponent is committed but not fully supported. In sword work, this would be the moment when your partner has begun to execute a cut and is so far into it that they can't pull it back. They have committed the sword and their body to the attack. If you merely evade, they will finish and their body will return to a stable condition as both feet settle back on the ground and the sword stops moving. In grappling, an example happens every time someone takes a step. Every step involves transferring your weight forward onto a foot that then touches the ground. You have to transfer the weight before the foot is on the ground though. This creates an instant when your weight is committed but not supported. If something happens in that instant, you can't pull it back or move it further forward easily or smoothly.

It is this instant when you're vulnerable. Understanding and recognizing this moment in your partner makes good timing possible. If you don't understand this, good timing is just good luck.

Learning to recognize and exploit moments when you partner or opponent is vulnerable takes practice. There are least two ways to recognize when that moment exists.

The first way is to learn to see it. Watch people move. Start by watching their feet, then see if you can understand what their feet are doing from watching their hips, and then try to understand where their feet are while only watching their chests, then their shoulders, then their heads. Eventually you'll be able to see the subtle shift in the body that occurs as the feet are moving and the weight is transferred to the unstable, moving foot. That's the moment to do something.

The other way to learn to recognize that movement is through touch. To quote the great judo coach Obi-Wan Kenobi, "Your eyes can deceive you." Just as bad, your eyes are also slow. If you are at touching distance, you need to sense what is happening faster than your eyes can tell you. You need to be able to feel it. I have spent, and continue to spend, a great deal of time walking around the *dojo* with my eyes closed and lightly touching my partner's arm or shoulder or lapel. We walk around and I practice maintaining the connection and moving with my partner while tracking exactly where their feet are. Occasionally, I reach out with my foot and lightly push my partner's foot while it's in the air. That's if I sense things correctly. If I don't I'm pushing on a foot that's on the ground and stable, or I'm pushing on a foot that isn't committed yet and floats away from me (often into a smooth counterattack). We walk around with me refining my ability to sense my partner's movement and occasionally pushing on her feet while she makes sure I don't walk into anything. Then we trade roles and I walk around with my eyes open while she practices catching my feet at just the right moment.

It amazes new students that I can walk around with my eyes closed and slide their feet out from under them. No peeking and no secret powers. From my hand on their sleeve or collar, I can feel where their feet are. It's not a secret power though. It's nothing more than learning to use your sense of touch more fully. Students learn the basics of this skill remarkably quickly. Within ten minutes, most students start to sense the foot movements, and to their surprise, they can feel their partner's moving foot even with their eyes closed. Feeling the right moment to catch the moving foot though, that takes a lot more practice. I'll let you know how much when I can do it every time.

Lately, I've started trying to understand my partner's movement when my ability to touch is extended through a weapon. I'm sure it is possible, and I can feel some of it, but I'm right back at the beginning of the learning curve with this. Our weapons are crossed and I can feel the strength and energy my partner puts into the sword or the staff. Just like when I was a beginning judo student though, I still can't interpret what I'm feeling. I want to fall back on my eyes. So here I am, once again a beginner slowly trying to figure things out, and probably overthinking things to a remarkable degree.

Timing is simple. Attack when your opponent isn't stable or can't move to defend themselves. At striking and weapons ranges, this might include stealing a few inches of *ma'ai* so that you can attack faster than they can respond. When grappling, it can be feeling that moment when their movement is committed but not yet supported. Rolling on the ground requires at least as acute a sense of balance and commitment as standing.

"Simple" doesn't mean "easy", though. It means "not complicated." "Easy" is something I've never encountered in the *dojo*. I keep working at the timing. I'm collecting bruises right now as I work on training myself to not move too soon when someone attacks with a weapon. I stand there watching the sword come up and down and at me and wait and wait and move at the last possible moment when they can't change the direction of the attack and can't even stop it. That's the goal anyway. Often what happens is that my lizard brain shrieks and I move too soon. Or the lizard brain forgets to say anything and I get clocked in the head while watching the sword come in.

If I manage the timing properly, my movements can look almost lazy because my partner can't do anything about them. I can move slow and smooth like I should. Good timing means never having to rush because there is nothing your partner can do about it at that moment. Timing lets you make the very most of your structural strength and flexibility and to use that spacing you control to the greatest advantage.

It's simple, but it's not easy. The right time is when your partner is committed to one direction and unable to stop. Add some energy at that moment. Move their foot a few inches. Add a little energy in the direction they are already going. Done at the right time, this is devastating even as it looks like you haven't done anything. Great timing is not the art of doing something at the right moment. Great timing is the art of already being there.

Note 1. The jodo *kata* Midare Dome can be seen at https://www.youtube.com/watch?v=34lVCEFI7Ms.

Note 2. A video of *de ashi barai* techniques can be seen at https://www.youtube.com/watch?v=EvWmNeSzs_Q.

PHILOSOPHY

Oddly enough, this is what drew me to budo in the first place. I was looking for an active expression of the ideas in the *Tao Te Ching*. The philosophy and values of budo are expressed in what we practice and how we practice it. Budo is concrete philosophy. The act of training in Kodokan Judo is to physically practice and literally experience the philosophy of the art. The same is true of iaido, kyudo, karatedo, and every other form of budo. Budo philosophy is one in which active practice and physical exploration is far more important than what is written or said. That doesn't make words worthless; it puts the emphasis on the practice. Words, such as these essays, are meant to supplement and support practice and help us understand what to focus on in our physical exploration of the philosophy of budo.

Figure 8: Nito demonstration at Kashima Shrine. Photo copyright Grigoris Miliaresis 2014.

THE ONLY THINGS I TEACH ARE HOW TO WALK AND HOW TO BREATHE

So you've decided to learn a martial art, and by some cosmic mischance you end up in my *dojo*. You'll probably be disappointed when I tell you that the only things I really teach are how to walk and how to breathe. This is ridiculous, since everyone over the age of eighteen months can do both, and by the time you wander into my *dojo* you've probably got more than twenty years of experience doing them, right? You probably think you're pretty good at both. I beg to differ. You're probably lousy at them. Breathing and walking are the foundations of all movement in the martial arts, but almost nobody spends enough time practicing them. The only people I know who spend time practicing breathing correctly are wind musicians and vocalists. I don't know anybody who practices walking properly. Everyone just assumes that they walk and breathe properly because they do both all day long.

The truth is that most of us have no clue how to breathe properly, and we walk like gorillas with leg cramps. Good breathing is fundamental to everything we do, and yet most of us have no idea how to do it. Ask a tuba player or flautist how to breathe and you will get a simple but valuable education. Breath comes from moving the diaphragm but I can't tell you how many martial artists I see breathing by moving their shoulders up and down or flexing their chests. That's bad technique, and if you can't breathe properly you wind up out of breath and unable to do much of anything. You certainly won't be able to coordinate and integrate your body into a single unit. It will stay a disparate bunch of parts until you learn to breathe.

You can't really be balanced if you're not breathing properly. And if you're not balanced, you're not walking and moving properly. And if you're not walking and moving properly, you won't be able to do anything that is taught in the *dojo*.

Musicians spend a lot of time working on proper breathing. I teach students to understand what proper breathing feels like by having them lie on the floor on their backs. In this position you cannot breathe with your shoulders or your chest. You have to breathe with your diaphragm. Lying on their backs, students can put their hands on the stomachs and really know what it feels like to breathe properly from the diaphragm. Then they can get up and practice replicating the experience while standing. At first, they have to feel with their hands if they are using their diaphragm and stomach properly, but after a while, they know the feeling well enough to recognize it without sticking their hands on their bellies. To check for shoulder breathing, they can look in a mirror. If they see their shoulders move when they breathe, they know they are doing it wrong.

It takes quite a while for this method of breathing to become habitual. After decades of bad breathing habits, proper breathing does not come naturally. The body will default to whatever habits it has developed over the years, so it will take conscious intervention to correct and ultimately change the habits. Initially, someone learning to breathe won't notice they are breathing wrong except in class when it is consciously called to their attention. Over time, as they become more familiar with the exercise and comfortable with the feeling, they will start to notice outside of practice when they aren't breathing properly and self-correct. Eventually, proper breathing will become their default breathing method.

That's a lot of work just to learn a different way of breathing than the one that has served just fine since you were born. So why bother? First, diaphragmatic breathing is more efficient than chest breathing or shoulder breathing. Your lungs expand more so you can take in more oxygen with each breath. Second, diaphragmatic breathing keeps the body together in a single unit. To breathe from your shoulders or chest, you have to loosen the connections between your shoulders and chest to the muscles in your back and abdomen so they can float up and out to let your lungs expand and take in oxygen. In doing so you are shifting your balance up and out. Breathing from your diaphragm doesn't involve shifting chunks of your body around. Your stomach is built to expand and contract without changing your balance or rearranging big pieces of you around.

Once you can breathe properly, you'll be able to relax into your body more effectively. When you stop throwing your chest and shoulders around with each breath, you can learn to connect with the ground through your legs and feet. As I said above, you can't really be balanced if you're not breathing properly. And if you're not balanced, you're not walking and moving properly. And if you're not walking and moving properly, you won't be able to do anything else that is taught in the *dojo*.

So now you've learned to breathe properly, and hopefully we've got you standing still in a nice, relaxed, stable posture. Now it's time for the tough part: learning to walk. Just because you can get from place to place without falling over every third step, it does not mean you are good at walking. Breathing can be done while lying down and standing still. Walking requires coordinating everything you've learned about breathing while actually moving your whole body. This is tougher than it sounds, and since even the <u>Mayo Clinic has a page</u> about it, I've discovered I'm not the only one concerned about this.

The basic walking method for naked house apes like us is to extend a foot and then fall forward onto it. Watch a toddler who has just learned how to walk, and this becomes very clear. They really are falling forward and catching themselves with every step. This is fine if you are eighteen months old and just figuring out how to get around on two legs, but if you want to do anything more than that, you'll need to refine the technique a bit.

The two basic walking movements in the arts I do are *ayumiashi* and *suriashi* (roughly, "walking feet" and "sliding feet"). Both of them require moving as a connected whole without throwing your balance into the air with each step. Start with the balanced, relaxed posture you have when breathing properly. Your head is up (the tai chi guys describe it as feeling like it is hanging from a thread, which is such a good description that I'm stealing it). Your back is straight and relaxed, your shoulders are not slumped forward and your back isn't pulled into an excessive arch. Everything sits naturally above your hips, and your hips sit comfortably atop your legs without any tension required to stay there.

Now move your leg forward driving it from the hips and without swinging your hips forward. Your hips should stay under your shoulders. Shoulders and hips should stay square and not rock from side to side or swing forward from right to left with each step. Your foot should not be so far forward that your weight comes crashing down on it. The transfer of weight should be smooth as the foot rolls from heel to toe. This is *ayumiashi*, regular walking, and just like breathing, it can take a bit of practice to make consistent even when you're not thinking about it.

Suriashi is a sliding foot movement where the ball of the foot never comes more than a hair's breadth off the floor (I was going to talk about the thickness of a sheet of rice paper, but that's been done).

This is not normal walking. This method of walking has an important place in training and learning to move for budo though. To manage it, bend your knees slightly, sink your hips a little and extend your right foot forward a bit. This time, instead of reaching out with the front foot, as in *ayumiashi*, drive your whole body forward as one unit by pushing with the left leg and the ball and toes of the left foot while keeping your body stable and balanced over the right leg. Do this all the way across the room. Now do it with the left foot forward.

Now, since I know you were holding your breath while you focused on doing the movements properly, try doing them while breathing. Once you can breathe properly and walk correctly you'll be ready to start learning budo. When you move and breathe well, your body becomes a single whole, with every part of you supporting every other part in accomplishing whatever you set out to do. If you aren't breathing and walking well, you aren't balanced and you don't have a solid platform upon which to build techniques. Instead, you have a base like a pile of sand. You can't learn to do anything budo related until you have a solid foundation that doesn't rock like a sailboat in high seas.

Now that you now longer move like a pregnant musk ox, we can start doing fun stuff like swinging swords and sticks and throwing people. None of these work when you are off-balance and huffing to get a breath. All of them require a body and breath that are fully integrated and working to support each other. If any part of the body or breath are out of whack, it will be readily apparent to your teacher, and eventually, to you too.

BUDO EXPECTATIONS AND REALITIES: UNDERSTANDING THE LIMITS OF WHAT WE STUDY

Budo. We all train in different arts. We all have expectations and ideas about what our arts teach us. It's easy for us to imagine that the techniques we study are applicable anywhere, and that if we practice diligently, we can use our skills against anything. We love to believe that what we study is the greatest art in the world. We tell ourselves how strong the techniques we study are, how effective they are, and how they will beat everything else. It doesn't matter if the art is judo or hapkido or Brazilian Jujutsu or savate or escrima or whatever. We like to believe that what we study is the absolute best.

I've been doing this martial arts stuff long enough that I've learned that "best" is a highly relative concept. A good friend, when asked if the martial art he teaches is the best martial art, replies, "No, thermonuclear warfare is the best martial art." He makes a number of good points with that answer. For a martial art to be "the best," what does it have to do? If you're going to war, almost everything is better than hand-to-(probably empty) hand martial art.

Each martial art teaches different things with a different focus. I train in a sword art that teaches a particular way to use a sword, one that helps to maximize the range of the sword. The sword is the core of this art. A friend of mine trains in a different art, one that uses a different set of body mechanics to wield the sword. The way his art does it gives a significantly smaller reach with the same length of sword. However, it maximizes the learning and usefulness of the core of his art, which is jujutsu. The principles that guide the body mechanics are the same for his jujutsu and his swordwork. This makes the learning much more effective. He doesn't have to learn one way to move while unarmed, and a different way to move while armed, and he doesn't risk mixing movement systems under stress. The sword movement may not be optimal for the sword, but the movement is optimal for teaching effective movement and action across a range of applications. Which is "best" then?

I have trained in judo for a long time and studied the knife defenses and counter attacks in the Kime No *Kata* and the Kodokan Goshin Jutsu. I thought these were really great. Then I started studying how to use weapons, and I became much less impressed with my skills against weapons. I discovered there were all sorts of things about weapons that are critical if you want to be effective against them. The first being understanding how something is really used. When I trained in techniques for use against weapons in judo, I was training with other *judoka*, not with people who were skilled with the weapons in question.

When I started training in weapons arts with people who were skilled with weapons, my understanding of the range and speed that particular weapons function at changed dramatically. What I had been doing before turned out to be little more than us imagining how a knife or stick or sword is used and then practicing against what we had imagined. When I started working with people who knew how to use those weapons, I discovered that their effective ranges were lot longer than I had imagined and that they were much faster than I had thought. I had to throw out pretty much everything I had practiced and start over, using actual knowledge upon which to build my training. That's pretty humbling. I thought I was reasonably good, and I had to admit that I was worse off than a beginner because I had learned a lot of things that were nothing less than completely wrong.

I'm guessing that this is not an uncommon issue, especially in *gendai* martial arts. Lots of modern arts teach defenses against a host of weapons without really teaching how those weapons are actually used, so even when people do paired practice, the lessons are not effective. This is what happened to me in judo. In *koryu* budo, the systems only train with weapons that they teach the use of, and the person doing the attacking is always the senior. This takes care of two issues: they don't develop illusions about being able to handle weapons outside of those they teach, and their study is always directed by someone who really knows the weapons to be trained.

There used to be an incredible seminar held every year in Guelph, Ontario. Kim Taylor would gather senior teachers from all sorts of *koryu* arts. Each would teach a two-hour introductory class about their art and then spend the rest of the weekend learning side by side with you in other teachers' classes. It was a rare treat and a chance to get a taste of how all sorts of arts and weapons are used, from jujutsu stuff to swords to 10 ft spears. The teachers all knew their stuff and quickly knocked any illusions we had about how things worked out of our heads. I vividly remember a high-ranking *aikidoka* saying after a sword class, "I thought I knew swordwork." He was admitting to himself that what he had studied in the aikido *dojo* about swords was very incomplete. He certainly wasn't the only person to walk out of one of those classes with the shards of previously held conceptions tinkling at the base of his mind. I had quite a few ideas rendered into old junk in a jujutsu class with Karl Friday of Kashima Shinryu. I just wish we'd been practicing on mats instead of in a dance studio.

I've discovered training with people who really know their weapons is critical. It is possible to work out effective ways to deal with weapons you aren't expert with, but I really don't want to experience all the pain that goes with that sort of learning curve, and I can't recommend it to anyone else, because usually, the only way to find out you're wrong is the really hard way. Working with someone who knows how to use a weapon properly means you don't chance developing inappropriate habits and techniques. A teacher or partner who knows the weapon will disabuse you of any incorrect ideas as soon as they see them.

I'm not saying one should not try anything new. Just do it smart. Work with someone who really knows the subject, so you don't make mistakes that can have unpleasant consequences. Train with your eyes open, and try to realize the real limits of what you know. Kim Taylor's seminars were an incredible experience because they were a chance to dive into our ignorance and find out just how small our islands of knowledge really are.

For now, I love going to the *dojo* and discovering more about myself. I love pushing myself to do things that are physically and mentally challenging. I love working with all the people I train with to mutually reach a higher level than the one we are on today. I love learning about myself and learning how to push myself to do things that are mentally and personally challenging outside the *dojo*. I love learning how to reshape my mind over time so that I can be a better me each day than I was the day before. All these things motivate me to get up and get to the *dojo* as much as I can.

WILL BUDO TRAINING MAKE ME A BETTER PERSON?

Will budo make me a better person? Not necessarily. Maybe if you want it to. If you train properly. There is an old idea that training in a Way (budo, sado, kado, etc.) will make you a better person. It's wonderful story: a lifetime of training has made the grizzled old teacher wise, kind, and gentle, and if we study the art, we too will be transformed into wise, kind, gentle people as well.

If only it were so.

You will become what you train to be. It is entirely possible to study and master the techniques of an art and completely miss its essence. This is perhaps most visible in international judo. If you watch international judo competitions, you can see some spectacular and subtle application of judo techniques and physical principles. The throws and techniques are incredible. The behavior of the contestants is no better than in any other sport though. There are good competitors who treat everyone with respect. There are bad sports who throw temper tantrums when they don't like the referee's calls. There are glory hounds who dance and shout and put on displays when they win. There jerks who are disdainful toward everyone around them.

With as many years of judo training and dedication as it takes to becoming a competitor at the international level, if just training in judo was going to make you a better person, all of these people should be fabulous human beings with grace, kindness, respect for everyone, and dignity, especially when on display in an international event. Instead, the behavior you see is no better than at any other sporting event. We can see clearly that spending years practicing a form of budo will not automatically transform you into a great person.

The focus of training in the *dojo* is usually on technique. It is entirely possible to study the techniques of an art, become extremely good at the techniques, and never touch the rich principles that animate the art and make it applicable throughout life and not just in the *dojo* or in a fight. Focusing on technical practice is appropriate, since the techniques are there to point you in the direction of the principles.

Chuang Tzu talks about the finger and the moon. The pointing finger directs us to the moon, but once we have found the moon we forget about the finger. If we fixate on the finger we will never move beyond it and will never find the moon. In budo, the techniques are like the finger. They point us toward the principles, but it is easy to become fixated on the techniques and miss their connections to deeper principles and ideas.

We train in techniques. That's how we learn budo. Techniques and *kata* teach us the fundamentals of the art and how to apply them. The techniques of an art are powerful. In judo, the throws, joint locks, and strangles are powerful and impressive. In other arts, there are strikes and weapons to study and be fascinated by. It's easy to get caught up in learning these techniques. The deeper, more subtle principles that make the techniques work can be forgotten in the race to master the techniques. This is especially true in something like judo or karate, where victory in competition can become a goal that eclipses and outshines everything else.

The techniques alone can seem powerful. Victory in competition brings glory and personal satisfaction. But these are not the principles of the art being studied, and they have nothing to do with becoming a better person. In fact, they more often lead in the opposite direction. The techniques of budo are dangerous and powerful. It's easy to get caught up with learning how to be dangerous and powerful. Knowing those dangerous and powerful techniques can give a person confidence. On the other hand, a person can become focused on that sense of power and become obnoxious and bullying because they have some power. In arts with a competitive side, such as judo and kendo, the focus on winning competitions can consume a person's attention so that they forget all the other parts of the art. They can stop respecting anything but victory and cheerfully ignore and belittle any aspect of the art that doesn't directly contribute to victory in competition.

In both cases, a person can study an art for a lifetime, and that study will still never make them a better person. It might even make them less of a person. They can become proud, arrogant, rude, and unpleasant to been around, pretty much the opposite of what a well-developed *budoka* should be.

Because of this, the first step to becoming a better person through budo practice is to avoid the pitfalls. The pitfalls are inherent in the practice. Fortunately, the lessons for becoming a better person are there too. If you are willing to work at them to learn the principles the techniques point us toward, you can do a lot with yourself. You have to be willing to work at applying these lessons not only to how you fight, but to how you live.

Each art has a few principles that drive it and give it unique characteristics, but they all have some unavoidable similarities as well (the optimal use of the human body being something that doesn't change). In any budo, you develop stamina and endurance and the ability to suffer through tough training in order to improve. These are certainly not bad character traits. But they are more like a foundation, since they can also support all of the negative traits mentioned earlier.

The big questions are, "what do you want to get out of your training?" and "who do you want to become?" Budo training will make you a better person if you actively direct your training and apply it to becoming a better person. If you leave your training at the *dojo* door every day, it won't have much effect on you. If you take it with you, look around and see the similarities between budo and the rest of life and apply the *dojo* lessons about dealing with conflict to the conflicts in life, then your budo can be a tool for becoming a better person.

Budo isn't passively effective. You have to actively work at it. If you work with it, it will make you more patient and less liable to lose your temper, more peaceful, and much calmer. These are all lessons you can pick up in the *dojo*. You know you can't tense up when practicing with someone who is attacking you with a big stick. It just creates opportunities for her to whack you and slows you down. Now, can you apply that lesson when you are being attacked verbally? Can you keep calm and choose the best response, rather than tensing up and girding for a fight? Can you breathe calmly and peacefully?

Keeping your balance and maintaining a solid foundation from which to act is critical in budo. By keeping those physical lessons in front of you, can you teach yourself to maintain a good mental balance and not go rushing into arguments and not reel back from non-physical aggression? Can a *judoka* learn to apply the lesson of *ukemi* and roll with the attack and not stiffen up? Can the *aikidoka* remember to get off the line of attack and realize that a counterattack may not even be necessary? Can the *kendoka* lightly deflect the incoming attack so it goes off into unoccupied space?

When you can start to do these things, you'll be on the path to applying your budo lessons to life and becoming a better person. Learning to apply these fundamentals can lead to the discovery of other budo lessons that you can train at in everyday life. One of the lessons of budo training is that you become good at what you practice. So, will budo training make me a better person? It will if that is what I train myself to be.

BUDO AS A "PROFESSIONAL SKILL" AND PROFESSIONALISM IN BUDO

Should budo teachers call themselves professionals? This is a discussion that comes up with fair regularity in modern and classical budo circles. There are a lot of people who see budo as a pure art form and equate accepting money for teaching as selling out the soul of the art. As an art form and classical legacy, budo should remain pure and above simple economics.

My early budo background is in Kodokan Judo, which in the USA, nearly has an allergy to professional instructors. There is a feeling common in judo and many classical budo circles that being a professional budo teacher requires that you sell out the core of your budo to attract a steady stream of students to pay the bills. The feeling is that, to make money, teachers have to quit teaching real budo and start doing marketing schemes and selling belts and ranks.

Then there is the example of Japan. There are very few professional budo teachers in Japan. Pretty much every city and town has one or more public *dojo* that anyone can rent for a very reasonable fee and hold a class. Nearly every town has a judo *dojo* and a kendo *dojo*, while cities may have several. (We won't even get into Tokyo and Osaka, which have so many judo and kendo *dojo* it would take years to visit them all). Many towns and cities also have a couple of *koryu* being taught as well. None of the teachers in these *dojo* is getting paid for teaching. The *dojo* communities are clubs where everyone gets together for the love of what they are doing. It doesn't hurt that even smaller towns will have several kendo seventh *dan*, and the judo club in even a small town will be run by a fifth *dan* or higher.

However, there *are* professional *budoka* in Japan. There aren't many, but they do exist. There are some professionals employed by the various local and regional governments to teach budo to the police. There is the wonderful example of the <u>Kokusai Budo Daigaku</u> (or International Budo University) that has a four-year degree program focused on the martial arts. It employs many people who are professional budo teachers and researchers. There are also a few professional instructors around who teach privately. Most of the ones I'm aware of teach karate or aikido.

What you don't have in Japan is a martial arts industry promoting business techniques for maximizing the cash flow generated by schools with a variety of schemes to get students to pay for extra classes and training. The budo teachers are professional teachers, not professional businessmen. The difference is, to me, an important one. Professional budo teachers are focused, maximizing the effectiveness of their teaching of budo. Professional businessmen focus on maximizing the profit of their business.

Every teacher I have dealt with in Japan never stops displaying professionalism. Professionalism is defined by Merriam-Webster's online dictionary as <u>"the skill, good judgment, and polite behavior that is expected from a person who is trained to do a job well."</u> It is something I have found lacking in many so-called teachers outside Japan. There are many teachers who do show professionalism outside Japan, but there are far too many who start teaching long before they have sufficient mastery to serve as examples of good technique, much less be able to communicate what students need to do. Just because you've got a colored belt doesn't mean you're ready to teach.

In fact, the organizations in Japan generally have a minimum rank for running your own *dojo*. In the Kendo Federation, it's fifth *dan*, and in the Judo Federation, it's fourth *dan*. Those are the minimums, but you don't see many *dojo* run by people with the minimum rank. The only time that happens is if an area doesn't have anyone else. Generally in the Kendo Federation, no one under seventh *dan* opens a *dojo*. In judo, that's usually fifth *dan*. You don't see people running out to start a *dojo*.

Running a *dojo* is considered a serious venture that calls for lots of experience. Outside Japan, fifth *dan* may sound like a high rank, but in Japan, it isn't. It barely gets you into the "serious student" category. People spend a lot of time developing their skills to the point where they can teach. Often, even after they open their own *dojo* they will make the journey a couple of times a week to train with their own teacher. I have to say, watching seventh *dan* working on things while an eighth *dan* makes corrections is a fabulous thing. They are all working at such a high level that it's gratifying if I can just figure out what the correction is.

Outside Japan, you see a lot of "teachers" who have stopped training, or at least their physical condition suggests that they aren't training very hard. If training and continual improvement is required for your students, it's required for you too. Budo teachers owe it to their students and to themselves to keep practicing, to keep training, to maintain their physical abilities and continue polishing themselves as examples of budo.

Oddly enough, I've never seen an example of teachers who stop training before their bodies give out in Japan. In fact, I see just the opposite. Teachers whose bodies are slowly fading still pushing themselves to get out on the floor and train, working hard to slow down the fading of their skills and discover something new about timing or spacing or control, and giving their students another lesson in perseverance. It's not about always being the best. It's about always giving our best.

This is what I would like to see more of. It's not about having a pretty belt and a nice title. It's about always working to give the best for our students. It really doesn't matter whether you are being paid money or not. Students are giving you a chunk of their time, their life. If a teacher is worrying about how to extract money from their students and is constantly coming up with new programs to sell to students, that's not professional. If a teacher is constantly working on improving their ability to transmit the fundamentals to their students and is working every day on improving her own fundamentals, that's a professional teacher.

BUDO TRAINING AND BUDO PHILOSOPHY

There is a lot of philosophizing that goes on in budo circles. I know that I am in the first rank of those guilty of it. There is far too much of philosophizing about budo by a lot of people who don't have the depth to do a good job of it. This might be a symptom of the Internet age though. Everyone who trains should be thinking about the ethics and values of budo, but not everyone's thoughts are ready for prime time. With the advent of the Internet bulletin board and personal blogs (like the one this book has emerged from), any fool (like me) can discourse to the world. That's probably not a great thing. However, budo without a philosophy of well-considered ethics and honor is just another way of hurting people, so I'm glad to see there is so much time and effort being put into thinking about it.

Having said that, I think you need a ratio of at least 100 to 1 of practice to philosophy, although it might need a lot more practice than that. Consider that the *Tao Te Ching* can be read in an hour, and then you can spend years discovering new stuff from it. All the good budo that I have encountered has been deeply thoughtful and filled with philosophical content, but the bulk of that content is written in the *kata* and application, not in words. The *kata* and application are structured so they teach nearly everything about an art, whether it is a *koryu bugei*, such as one of the branches of Yoshin Ryu jujutsu, or a modern art like Kodokan Judo or aikido.

The *kata* and applications practiced don't just teach how to do a technique. They teach what the art values and how it thinks as well. If you haven't studied the *kata* and application of the art deeply, any written or spoken lessons about the art will be meaningless. In Kodokan Judo, there are nine sets of *kata*, and they teach a full range of techniques for throwing, pinning, joint locking, choking, and disarming. But the techniques taught are just the beginning. The *kata* teach how to apply them from a variety of ranges and attacks, so you can also learn something about when to apply the technique.

When studied properly, the *kata* teach a student to see how close someone has to be before they are dangerous. The *kata* also teach an art's philosophy on how strongly to respond and what level of damage to inflict on an assailant. Some arts believe in preemptive strikes. (Muso Jikiden Eishin Ryu and Muso Shinden Ryu share the same assassination *kata* Tana No Shita. One of the first *kata* in Araki Ryu is an assassination *kata*.) Other arts don't include surprise attacks but are willing to strike first once they have been threatened (Shinto Muso Ryu's Tachi Otoshi). Still others refrain from action until actually attacked (Kodokan Judo). This is philosophy at a fundamental level that is embedded in the *kata* of the particular systems. These *kata* all make an ethical statement about what is acceptable behavior in the eyes of the people who crafted the system.

Studying an art's *kata* teaches you what the system approves of and disapproves of. It also teaches about things such as how strongly to respond to a given situation or provocation. Some systems always respond with lethal force (see pretty much any *koryu bugei* from before 1604 CE). Others have a variety of responses that range from killing or crippling an attacker down to simple restraint. Shinto Muso Ryu has a variety of responses in the kill, cripple, or seriously injure range, while arts like Kodokan Judo and aikido tend to focus on the range from causing injury down to simple restraint. These are all philosophical statements, but without deep practice of the art, the philosophy of the arts cannot truly be understood.

Most arts also have written or verbal teachings that supplement the physical training, but the physical training is the core of the system and really teaches what the system believes. The associated writings help one to better understand the art and provide some guidance in the form of things to think about while practicing. However, without intensive training in the system's *kata* and application, the writings and verbal teachings are nearly meaningless because they lack the proper context for understanding their intent.

Kano Jigoro *Shihan*, the founder of Kodokan Judo, famously crafted two guiding principles for his art:

Jita Kyoei (自他共栄), often translated as "Mutual Benefit And Welfare"
Seiryoku Zenyo (精力善用), often translated as "Maximum Efficiency Minimum Effort"

These are simple statements, but the true depth of their meaning and intent can only really be understood through intensive practice of the system that embodies their meaning. Mutual Benefit And Welfare sounds very nice, but actually practicing it in the *dojo* while you train is much more difficult than the simple phrase suggests. The dedicated student has to learn how to do this even when they don't like their training partner; even when they are tired, angry, or annoyed; and even when a partner may have actually harmed them in some way. The principle is not easy to implement, and it isn't meant to be applied just during *keiko*.

Seiryoku Zenyo is even more difficult to understand, though perhaps it is less emotionally difficult to implement. It starts out in technique but grows quickly after that. All Kodokan Judo students soon realize how important the principle is for performing the techniques of the system properly and effectively. That is quickly obvious when you see a sixty-year-old *judoka* doing *randori* with a twenty-year-old, and you notice that the sixty-year-old is relaxed and breathing easily while the twenty-year-old is stressed, stiff, and gasping for air. Same techniques, same art, but the sixty-year-old is doing a much better job of applying *Seiryoku Zenyo*. While the twenty-year-old tries to use strength and youthful energy, the sixty-year-old is doing only as much as is really necessary, resulting in the sixty-year-old being fresh and relaxed after a few minutes of *randori* while the twenty-year-old stands next to him exhausted and panting for breath. The difficult secret is that you are supposed to be able to scale the application of *Seiryoku Zenyo* to everything else you do in your life. It's not meant just to be hidden in the *dojo*. Without dedicated practice in the *dojo* though, the real depth of the concept will never be revealed. There are lots of things that seem efficient at first but that the trial and error of practice reveal to be mistakes.

As a student advances deeper and deeper into a budo school, they slowly discover more depth to the teachings, both the practical, physical teachings of the system and the written teachings. The core of any budo system is the physical teachings of the art, the *kata*. The writings associated with the art help a student to understand what is embodied in the *kata*, but without extensive practice of the *kata* and deep appreciation for their contents, the writings will just be so many scratches on paper. This is true whether they are Kano Jigoro's writings about mutual benefit and maximum efficiency; Ueshiba Morihei's writings about the circle, square, and triangle; Shinto Muso Ryu's *Shiteki Bunsho* about the nature of the *jo*; or some of the esoteric teachings of other styles like Yagyu Shinkage Ryu or Araki Ryu or Miyamoto Musashi's writings for Niten Ichi Ryu. If you haven't studied the physical portion of the curriculum deeply, the philosophy will be meaningless.

Now get out there in the *dojo* and study your art's philosophy!

HOW TO ADAPT AN ART FORM TO FIT YOU

I often hear people talk about making an art their own and adapting the art form to suit them. I hear it most often in reference to arts like aikido, karate, and judo. The discussion will turn to adapting the art to suit an individual. This is a quite reasonable question. After all, every student's body is different, with unique strengths and weaknesses. Adapting an art form to suit an individual just makes sense, particularly in the modern, eclectic world we live in.

In competitive judo, with dozens of legal throws, there is no way one person can be equally good at all of them. So people specialize in a couple of throws that they polish to perfection while giving the rest of the throwing techniques little more than cursory practice so they are familiar with what they look like and how they feel. For a competitor, there is little use in doing a lot of techniques at a mediocre level. What they need are a few techniques they can hit from anywhere during a match. A compilation reel of people doing a number of different versions of Tai Otoshi on YouTube gives a good feel for the ways and places in which one throw can be adapted for use.

I hear explicit discussion about adapting an art to individual practitioners quite often in aikido as well. People want to make aikido theirs. Even before the advent of YouTube, aikido students could see many different senior aikido teachers up close at seminars. There they could see that each of these teachers seemed to move a bit differently and have somewhat different approaches to practicing and doing aikido. From there, it's natural for a student to want to make the aikido they do as personal an expression of aikido as that done by the *shihan* they see at seminars.

Adapting the techniques of an art form to suit your particular body and personality is a reasonable idea. We all have different bodies with a variety of strengths and weaknesses, so why shouldn't we try to optimize the techniques we study for our bodies. We can tweak and adjust the way techniques are done so they work better for us and are easier to do. It seems reasonable that a person who is 6'4" (200 cm) tall will do their Tai Otoshi or Kotegaeshi or Iriminage differently from someone who is 5' (152 cm).

Across the spectrum of body types and shapes and sizes, students can see that they should be adapting their art to their particular body characteristics. Often they ask when they can or should start doing this. I've seen many comments that give a time after a student is well into *dan* (black belt) ranks. After someone reaches fourth *dan* in most *gendai* arts, they should have a really solid foundation in the art and be able to experiment without getting into trouble by teaching themselves mistakes. They can start making the art their own, and by the time they reach sixth or seventh *dan*, they could have a personal style that is clearly all their own.

This is great, right? You study the art, learn it, and then mold it to your body. I used to think it was great. Lately though, I've begun to wonder. I do both *gendai* budo (Kodokan Judo) and *koryu* budo (Shinto Hatakage Ryu and Shinto Muso Ryu). At one time, I thought that *koryu* budo could learn many things from the way *gendai* budo are taught and practiced. *Gendai* budo, particularly arts like judo with a huge global competitive aspect, constantly mine modern science for the latest training methods and techniques for improving competitor's skills and the efficiency of their training. I don't think anyone would argue that Ronda Rousey hasn't done an incredible job of adapting her competitive judo training to the world of mixed martial arts and demonstrated the effectiveness of it.

Competition is an exceptionally narrow set of conditions though. Conditions that can make techniques and stances that are foolish to try in other situations into perfectly reasonable responses. A classic example is the strongly defensive posture you can see in many competitive judo matches. It's very bent over and committed forward to block out your grappling partner. Outside the competitive match though, the position is rife with openings for punches, kicks, or small weapons attacks. This competitive defensive posture is quite effective for blocking out sporting attacks. It would be a huge mistake to try to apply this or any of the defensive tactics from competitive judo to a broader practice intended for budo. If you try to use that stance while doing any of the combative judo *kata*, you would discover all sorts of unpleasant general weaknesses in it. Competitive judo has adapted itself to the rules of competition. The International Judo Federation is constantly trying to tweak the rules to push competitors back toward a classical style of judo that is more broadly effective than just within the limited space of the competition area. The effectiveness of their efforts may be questionable, but their continued effort is praiseworthy.

Competitors only have to be concerned with the narrow range of possibilities present within the competition arena. Those of us doing martial arts as budo have a much broader world of possibilities and consequences to be concerned with. We've ruled out taking ideas from the rarified world of competition, but we still want to make our budo our own and adapt it to our unique body and personality. Now we can start looking at what there is that we can change without destroying the art.

Fundamental stances are essential in any art. This might be the first place that someone could modify the art to suit them. I like to look at leading practitioners of arts like judo, aikido, and kendo, arts where there is more opportunity to adapt an art to oneself without major criticism. Aikido and judo provide perhaps the best examples because there are plenty of high-level practitioners around to look at. Kendo leaves a bit less room for personalization, but it's still there.

Looking at aikido, I see people who prefer to work from *hanmi* stance and others who prefer a *shizen* (squared up, front facing, natural) stance. When they have the opportunity to reset their stance, they go back to their preferred stance. I don't see high-level teachers modifying their stances or coming up with new ones. They just have a stance they prefer to work from.

The same is true in judo (after we ignore all the bad defensive postures seen in judo competitions at all levels). People don't modify the basic stances and grips. Some people prefer a right-side grip, some a left-side grip, some higher, and others lower. What you don't see are people inventing new grips. With millions of people doing judo, and thousands of those practicing at elite national and international levels, if there were a new posture or grip that could be effective, I'm certain we'd have seen it. What we see are people fighting from the right or the left, or even squared up. Some big guys like higher grips, and occasionally you'll see someone who likes to fight with a sleeve and sleeve grip instead of a sleeve and collar grip. That's about the extent of stance and grip personalization you see in judo.

The problem with modifying fundamental stances is that they are just that: fundamental. If you start modifying them, then everything in the art that follows from those stances has to be modified to fit the new version of the stance. More problematic is that the stances have been chosen and refined within the art for their strength and flexibility. In any of the fully established arts I know, whether *koryu* or *gendai*, the stances have been refined to their essentials, and changing them just creates a weakness.

What could you change in any fundamental stance that wouldn't weaken it? Body angle, hip alignment, or foot position? If you change your body angle, then you're not aligned to deal with your attacker. If you shift your hip alignment, you lose the connection between your upper body, your hips, and your feet. Change your foot position and you can't react properly when an attack comes in.

So when you're personalizing your budo and putting your particular stamp on the budo you do, it looks like changes to stances aren't the way for people to go about it. Watching high-level practitioners shows that while they have stances they prefer, they don't make significant changes to them. I should also note that if you watch any of them long enough, they are generally quite competent in all the stances of their art; they just prefer some stances over others.

If people aren't putting their stamp on the art by modifying the stances of the art, how about the techniques? This is a tough one too. I can't imagine being able to monkey around with the essence of a technique like Harai Goshi or Shihonage and being able to make some modification that would let it work as well as the fundamental technique, at least not any modification that someone else hasn't already thought of.

The judo world is quite large, and I know a tiny, tiny fraction of it. But people have worked out a lot of different ways to attack Harai Goshi. I remember my first judo teacher telling us about how proud he had been of a variation on a throw he had come up with. He used it quite successfully in a tournament. After the tournament, one of the old guys came over to his teacher and complimented them on the beautiful technique. This old guy said he hadn't seen that version of the technique in ages, not since some Japanese guy had used it back in the 1930s. So much for doing something new.

The same holds true for something like Shihonage. I tried to find a nice compilation video, but no one seems to have made one yet. A search for "shihonage" on YouTube though brought up dozens of individual variations on the technique. If someone can think of a highly effective variation of Shihonage that is not already represented by a video on YouTube, I would be amazed and impressed.

All the various entries for Harai Goshi, and all the versions of Shihonage on YouTube, work because throughout the variations, the fundamental essence of the technique has not been changed. People can change how they enter, what movement they use for the setup, what attack they are responding to, what position they start in, and a dozen other things, but the core of what they are doing, the basic technique being applied, doesn't change.

When we see someone doing their version of an art like judo or aikido, we're not seeing a fundamentally different art. We're not even seeing an art that has been adapted to suit a particular person. What we're seeing is a person who has mastered the art and found particular pieces of it that they like and are most comfortable with, which they use more often than other parts of the art. Their personal "style" of aikido isn't a personal style at all. You're seeing the parts they like and are most comfortable doing.

An aikido teacher who usually starts from *hanmi* stance and does a lot of Shihonage in her demonstrations has not made any modifications to aikido to make it suit her. She's mastered it and chooses the stances and techniques that she likes best. A *judoka* who specializes in Tai Otoshi and can do it from fifteen different positions and entries is still a *judoka*. She's just become particularly proficient at one technique and is most comfortable with it. She's still a *judoka* and can still do the rest of the syllabus.

I started out with the question "How do you adapt your budo to yourself?" The answer is that you don't. You study your art. You master your art. Within it, you may find particular stances and techniques that you are exceptionally comfortable with and feel best when you do them. As you use these more and more, they will be viewed by others as your particular "style" of aikido (or judo or whatever). You'll still be doing the standard version or your art. You may have specialized in particular versions, but it's still aikido or judo. Other people see your particular emphasis in stances and techniques and mistake technical preferences as personal style and modifications to the art.

You haven't modified the art. You do the full art, but you are especially comfortable in particular stances and you find some techniques more accessible and easier to perform than others. There's nothing new there. That sort of thing is older than humanity. Even before Sun Tsu, people studied their opponents to learn the techniques, tactics, and strategy they preferred.

In fact, if you are too wedded to particular stances and versions of techniques, it makes you weaker, not stronger. People will know exactly what you're going to do and how you will do it. It's very easy to catch a tiger that walks down the same stretch of trail every day. You just keep laying traps for him. Eventually, one will work, especially if it capitalizes on the tiger using those same movements and habits.

So don't try to adapt your art to yourself. Recognize a truth that is evident in *koryu bugei*. You don't adapt an art to yourself. You adapt yourself to the art. Master the fundamental postures and techniques of the art you are studying. Make them a part of who you are so you can't possibly do them wrong. These fundamentals are the core of the art, and they are what make everything else in the art possible. They are designed to eliminate as many openings and weaknesses as possible. If you mess with them, you will be far more likely to do something that weakens you than something that strengthens you.

IS *KATA* TOO RIGID AND MECHANICAL?

Kata are mechanical and rigid. They teach petrified patterns and leave the person vulnerable if their partner does something different from the prescribed techniques. People who learn *kata* don't learn how to adjust spontaneously to new and different attacks. They become rigid in their responses and thus are easily beaten by anyone who is familiar with their preprogrammed responses and can use them as a trap. *Kata* don't teach you how to deal with anything other than the exact form of the *kata*.

People in Japan have been making these charges against *kata* training since at least the 1700s, and probably longer than that. These are the basic accusations made against *kata* practice. Then there are other narratives.

Kim Taylor recently reminded me of a story that I heard many years ago. As the story goes, two lines of a *koryu* art met at a big *embu* and decided to get together and train a little. Even though the lines had not trained together in something like 200 years and had developed different interpretations of the *kata*, it didn't take long at all for them to start doing the *kata* fast and hard.

Another friend recently recounted an instance when training with a senior partner who seemed to forget the *kata*, so he just went on with what seemed appropriate. My friend simply adjusted to the new attacks and continued on. After a few spontaneous attacks and responses, the senior found his footing in the *kata* and they wrapped things up.

So what's up? If *kata* practice is so rigid and promotes all the bad habits that it is charged with, why has it survived so long, and how could people adapt to scenarios like those above? Maybe, just maybe, the people criticizing *kata* practice don't do it well and don't how to use *kata* as a training tool. In particular, practitioners of modern sports styles that emphasize sparring and grappling competitions don't seem to understand what a *kata* is or how to use it.

The first thing to realize is that nearly all *kata* in Japanese systems (as opposed to Okinawan systems, which have an entirely different history) are paired practice. The primary exception to this is iai *kata* for drawing and handling a live sword. The problem there is that accidents from mistakes tend to be so severe, it is difficult to recruit new training partners. Pretty much everything else, including practice with stand-in swords for *kenjutsu*, is practiced in pairs, with an attacker and responder.

Kata critics get one basic fact correct: that *kata* are prescribed patterns of attack and response. From this basic starting point, they then proceed down a path that has little resemblance to what happens during actual *kata* practice. Critics of *kata* assume that because the basics of *kata*, which attack(s) and which response(s) are prescribed, that everything else in the *kata* is also prescribed. They assume that because one part is clearly defined, that all parts of the *kata* are clearly defined, and that is where they get it all wrong.

Kata are not rigid constructions where every movement is written in stone. The first thing that is open to variation is the timing. *Uchi*, the striker or attacker, is by traditional convention the senior. This is because the *uchi* controls the timing of each major attack against the *shitachi*, the person learning the weapon or empty hand skills. There is no set timing for the attacks. The *uchi* doesn't have to do the attacks all in the same timing and rhythm. If you happen to watch a relatively junior student doing the *shitachi* role, then the attacks of the *uchi* are likely to be clearly visible and easy to see coming. On top of that, the rhythm and timing of the attacks will be very straightforward. This is because the person is learning the basics of attack and response.

Once a student is past that basic level, which doesn't take long at all, things quickly get complicated and interesting. The first thing the *uchi* can do is play with the timing. Just because the *uchi* is within range for an attack doesn't mean they have to immediately attack. They can stand there and wait as long as they want, forcing the *shitachi* to really watch for the attack, maintaining focus and awareness the whole time. If the *uchi* notices the focus of the *shitachi* slipping, that's the moment to attack for maximum learning. Or the *uchi* can do something to draw the *shitachi* into acting before the *uchi* is committed to an attack, leaving the shitachi wide open for the *uchi*. (I've had several uncomfortable meetings with wooden swords and other weapons because I fell for this sort of thing.) These are prime teaching experiences.

The attack and response of the *kata* are prescribed. Nothing says that the *uchi* can't adjust when she attacks or specifies what movement she performs before attacking. Learning to only respond to a real attack is a significant lesson, and one that students learn in *kata* practice. If the *shitachi* is drawn into responding before she's attacked, that's something you have to learn to recognize. It takes a while to really learn to read someone's movement and intent, but that's one of the things you learn in good *kata* practice.

The *uchi* can also mess with the rhythm. As you get comfortable with the *kata*, there is a tendency for people to fall into a consistent rhythm. One of the responsibilities of the *uchi* is to change up the rhythm of the attacks so the *shitachi* stays alert and doesn't fall into the habit of thinking that the attack will always be at one speed and one timing. It's amazing how slipping a half or whole second pause into a *kata* can transform the rhythm, upend for the *shitachi* their grasp of the *kata* and self-control, and cause the *shitachi* to make a grave mistake that leaves them wide open to an attack from the *uchi*.

This leads to another misconception. The fact that attacks and responses in a *kata* are prescribed, doesn't preclude the *uchi* from stepping in to demonstrate a mistake the *shitachi* has made or a juicy opening they have left. The *uchi* isn't going to bash the *shitachi* in the head (I hope), but the *uchi* is likely to gently attack through the inviting gap the *shitachi* has left. How else would the *shitachi* learn to not make a particular mistake? I know I've moved only to discover a weapon tip an inch from my nose because, as *shitachi*, I didn't control the *uchi* properly, leaving a nice hole in my defense that my partner was more than happy to demonstrate for me.

There is a core technique in Shinto Muso Ryu called Hiki Otoshi Uchi. It involves striking your partner's sword so it is swept down, around, and behind them, putting them slightly off-balance for an instant. At least, that's what happens if you do it right. I can't count the number of times I have done Hiki Otoshi Uchi, expecting to flow into the opening left by the missing sword, only to find the sword has somehow gotten to a spot where it was about to run up my nose! There is nothing in *kata* practice that says your partner has to let you get away with a weak technique. If your partner is allowing you to use a weak technique, he is doing it wrong. *Kata* is the perfect place to find out you are doing something wrong.

In addition, *kata* practice is perfect for the endless "what if" questions students ask. If a student asks, "what if I do this?" or "what if my *uchi* is stronger/bigger/dumber/etc.?," *kata* provides a great, controlled environment for students to explore these options. Of course, if they ask about something completely different, it's always reasonable to say, "We're working on this *kata* right now. What you're asking is completely different. We'll get to a *kata* that deals with that another time."

There are lots of moments in the *kata* of the systems I study where it's quite reasonable to wonder why the *uchi* or *shitachi* don't do something different. I've asked these questions, and usually the *sensei* doesn't bother explaining. He just says, "OK, try it." We do the *kata* with my variation, and I discover a sword in my ribs, a fist in my nose, the floor smacking me between the shoulder blades, or some other equally unpleasant result. Then the *sensei* will go on to show me what he did. Later, I usually grab a fellow student and we play with it until we can create the response *sensei* used for us too.

Koryu bugei kata are a framework for learning that people have been working with, tweaking, and testing for hundreds of years. They can certainly stand the pressure of students pushing and pulling on them to see if they are sturdy. If students have questions, they should be playing with and testing the *kata*. They will find the answers. I know I've seen my teachers play with *kata* and technique when someone asks a really interesting question.

Then, of course, there is the recurring problem of beginners mixing *kata* and doing something other than what is in the *kata*. Seniors don't seem to have any problem adjusting to these impromptu changes to the *kata*. It happens quite frequently. It even happens that senior people will do something other than the *kata* from time to time, and if their partner can't respond, they may get hurt.

The most amusing complaint about *kata* from many people is that they are an old-fashioned, out-of-date training method. Yet the same people will talk endlessly about their great training drills.

What's funny about modern sports stylists criticizing *kata* training is that the bulk of their training is *kata* style training; they just don't realize it because they call it by different names. Guess what the word for "training drill" is in Japanese? *Kata.* Look at the sequence in any training drill video. The practice of those nice, controlled prescribed attacks against a specific defense are *kata.* Depending on the skill of the people involved, the practice will be faster or slower. Just like in martial arts *kata.* People in modern martial arts are constantly refining their training drills to improve their training. *Koryu* martial artists have been refining their *kata* for centuries. It's no surprise they've got them down to a solid set.

Kata are teaching and learning tools. There is room in them for playing with speed, timing, distance, and even different responses. If all you do is numbly repeat a set pattern at the same speed, rhythm and intensity, you aren't doing *kata* training.

ABOUT PETER BOYLAN

Peter has been studying Japanese martial arts for over thirty years. He started with Kodokan Judo while in college and added iaido and jodo after moving to Japan, where he lived and studied for nearly seven years. Currently, he is a fifth *dan* in All Japan Kendo Federation iaido, fifth *dan* in All Japan Kendo Federation jodo, third *dan* in Kodokan Judo, and holds a *Shomokuroku* in Shinto Muso Ryu and a *Jun Shihan* certificate in Shinto Hatakage Ryu. When asked about interests outside of budo, he seemed estranged to that idea.

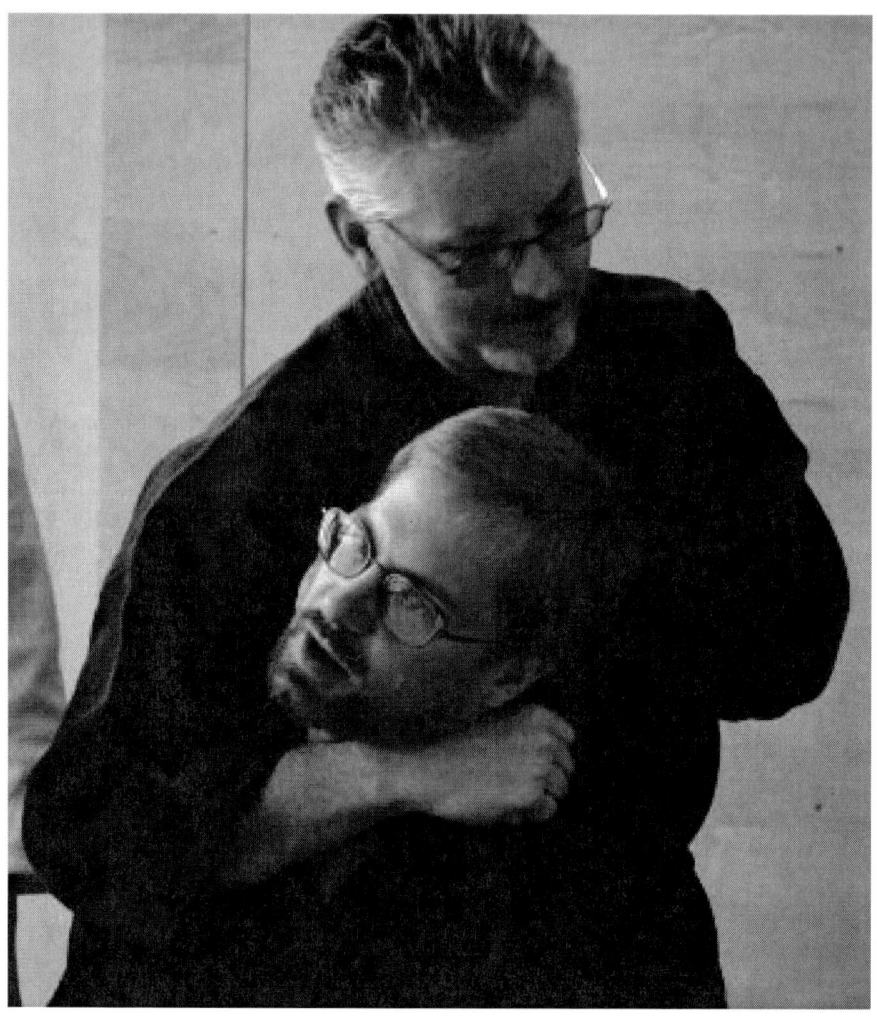

*Figure 9: Peter Boylan about to be choked by Chuck
Gordon. Photo copyright Peter Boylan 2016.*